MAKING THE GRADE WITH A+DD

A Student's Guide to Succeeding in College with Attention Deficit Disorder

D0036013

STEPHANIE MOULTON SARKIS, PH.D.

New Harbinger Publications, Inc.

Publisher's Note

Care has been taken to confirm the accuracy of the information presented and to describe generally accepted practices. However, the authors, editors, and publisher are not responsible for errors or omissions or for any consequences from application of the information in this book and make no warranty, express or implied, with respect to the contents of the publication.

The authors, editors, and publisher have exerted every effort to ensure that any drug selection and dosage set forth in this text are in accordance with current recommendations and practice at the time of publication. However, in view of ongoing research, changes in government regulations, and the constant flow of information relating to drug therapy and drug reactions, the reader is urged to check the package insert for each drug for any change in indications and dosage and for added warnings and precautions. This is particularly important when the recommended agent is a new or infrequently employed drug.

Some drugs and medical devices presented in this publication may have Food and Drug Administration (FDA) clearance for limited use in restricted research settings. It is the responsibility of the health care provider to ascertain the FDA status of each drug or device planned for use in their clinical practice.

Distributed in Canada by Raincoast Books

Copyright © 2008 by Stephanie Moulton Sarkis
New Harbinger Publications, Inc.
5674 Shattuck Avenue
Oakland, CA 94609
www.newharbinger.com

Cover design by Amy Shoup; Text design by Michele Waters-Kermes; Acquired by Melissa Kirk; Edited by Karen O'Donnell Stein

---

Library of Congress Cataloging-in-Publication Data

Sarkis, Stephanie.
  Making the grade with add : a student's guide to succeeding in college
with attention deficit disorder / Stephanie Moulton Sarkis.
      p. cm.
  Includes bibliographical references and index.
  ISBN-13: 978-1-57224-554-9 (pbk. : alk. paper)
  ISBN-10: 1-57224-554-9 (pbk. : alk. paper) 1. Attention-deficit-
disordered youth--Education (Higher) 2. College student orientation.
I. Title.
  LC4713.2.S27 2008
  371.94--dc22
                    2008016256

15   14   13

10   9   8   7   6   5   4   3

To all of my clients and patients who are navigating the college seas.

Contents

Acknowledgments

Thank you to Katie Porter Marshall for coming up with the idea for this book. Thank you to Elias Sarkis, MD, for his recommendations, assistance, and support. Thank you to all of the college students who offered their tips and recommendations, especially Nathalie Demirdjian. Thank you to my editors at New Harbinger, Melissa Kirk and Jess Beebe, for their feedback and support. Thank you to all of my friends and family who offered support, including Janice Moulton, Claude Moulton, William Moulton, Christine Whitney, Henry Sarkis, Yvonne Sarkis, Jason Bianchi, Jennifer Frazier, Toby Sarkis, and Lucy Sarkis.

Introduction

So you've decided to go to college (or you are there already). You may be feeling a combination of excitement, independence, liberation, trepidation, fear, and even sheer terror. All of those feelings are normal. When you have ADD, those feelings can be amplified, in part due to past experiences with school and concerns about being totally responsible for yourself for the first time. But rest assured: you *can* have a successful and fun college experience.

In this book, you'll find tips and suggestions specifically geared toward college students with ADD. College presents a different set of issues for people with ADD. You may need to study differently than your friends do, or you may need to have a different living situation—one with fewer distractions and more flexibility. You may be planning on taking medication for your ADD while you're at college. This book covers those issues and more. Although the book is focused on students who are going away to school for the first time, the tips contained in the book can help all college students, regardless of their year in school or major. Keep in mind that what works for some people with ADD may not necessarily work for you. Take a "use it or leave it" approach to this book. If something works for you, great! If something doesn't work for you, leave it, move on, and try something else.

Are you entering college at an older-than-traditional age? Perhaps you've already been in the workforce for a considerable amount of time; maybe you already have a family of your own. You're not alone: it's very common for people with ADD to start (or restart) college later in life. Much of the book is geared toward young adults, but you can find plenty of information that is just as applicable to you.

Let's take a look at the topics covered in the book. Chapter 1 is an overview of ADD, how it affects the college experience, and how to find a college that fits you. Chapter 2 gives information about housing, roommates, transportation, and how to keep your stuff organized in a small space. Chapter 3 will discuss class schedules, professors, and choosing a major. Chapter 4 gives tips on taking tests and clues you in to the best study methods. Chapter 5 contains information about your rights as a college student with ADD, what services are available to you on campus, and how to advocate for yourself. Chapter 6 discusses medication options for the treatment of ADD. Chapter 7 discusses health issues, including self-care and wellness. Chapter 8 contains information on how to manage your money on your own, including budgeting, concerns about credit cards, and keeping track of your finances. Chapter 9 gives information about the social aspects of college—how to get involved in helpful activities, and what activities to avoid. In addition, chapter 9 offers help for students who feel that their ADD has prevented them from having satisfying relationships. Chapter 10 contains information on life after college—graduate school, resumés, interviews, and getting an ADD-friendly job in the "real world." Throughout the book, college students with ADD will share their experiences and give you recommendations. At the end of the book, you'll find a list of resources so you can get the most out of your college experience.

After reading this book, you'll be more informed about the following:

- Your ADD diagnosis

- How ADD affects your college experience

- Finding the right college for you

- Keeping organized in a small space

- Getting along with roommates

- Finding a major that keeps your interest

- Where and how to study

- Advocating for yourself

- Safeguarding your medications

- Managing your money

- Balancing your school and social life

- Preparing yourself for life after college

1

Your New Adventure

It's a fairly widespread assumption, even today, that ADD is something you "grow out of." However, 4.4 percent of adults in the United States have ADD. That's 8 million people! (Kessler et al. 2006). Approximately 50 percent of children retain their ADD symptoms in adulthood (Wilens 2004). Adults with ADD are less likely to attend college than people without ADD (Biederman et al. 2006). By thinking about or enrolling in college, you're already ahead of the curve! In this chapter, you will learn about the challenges that college students with ADD face. You'll also learn what adult ADD looks like, and how to find a college that best suits you.

HOW ADD ALTERS THE COLLEGE EXPERIENCE

People with ADD may be successful in high school, but many find they have difficulties in college. There are a few reasons for this. First, students have a lot more unstructured time in college—sometimes two or maybe even three hours between classes. You don't have someone helping you to adhere to a daily schedule—your mother won't be telling you that you have to finish your schoolwork before you can go out with your friends. It is up to you to determine how to structure your time.

Second, the atmosphere of college is more competitive than it is in high school. If you were at the top of your graduating class in high school, you are now in classes with a bunch of people who were also at the top of their graduating class. In addition, some professors grade on a curve, which means they grade you based on how your performance compares to that of the other students in the class, which can create a competitive atmosphere. Since people who have ADD are more prone to frustration and self-doubt, this can throw you for a loop. However, there is also a positive side to the competition: having all these motivated people around you can make your classes and friendships much more interesting.

Students with ADD may also have difficulties adapting to college due to lower self-esteem and the feeling that they have fewer social skills than non-ADD students (Shaw-Zirt et al. 2005). You also may not have the daily face-to-face access to your friends and family members who would usually help you stay focused or cheer you on when you get stuck or frustrated. But one of the great things about college is that you can form a new support system and still keep your support system at home.

Risks of Young Adults with ADD

Certain behaviors and issues come up more frequently when you are a young adult with ADD. The ADD brain craves excitement and novelty, and some of the behaviors that go along with filling that need can be detrimental to your physical health and general well-being. Young adults with ADD are more likely than others to experience the following:

- Alcohol, tobacco, and drug abuse

- Depression, anxiety, and suicide

- Lack of friends

- Debt

- Auto accidents

- Unplanned pregnancies and sexually transmitted diseases

- Dropping out of college

- Unemployment or lower income than that of peers

- Legal problems

The above list may strike you as pessimistic or over the top, but being aware of these risks can help prevent these things from happening to you.

SYMPTOMS AND CAUSES OF ADULT ADD

You may have been diagnosed with ADD when you were a child. Your parents may have had you evaluated for ADD because you had difficulty staying in your seat, didn't follow directions, often injured yourself doing daredevil stunts, or weren't working to your potential in school. You may have been prescribed medication that you still take today.

When you have ADD as an adult, it looks different from the ADD you had when you were a child. Your brain has matured since you were a child, but it does not lose its "ADD-ness." You may just be less hyperactive now that you are older. Instead of getting out of your seat in class, you may feel a sense of internal restlessness. Instead of climbing on the furniture at home, you may have a strong need to engage in outdoor activities. Other signs of adult ADD include:

- Hyperfocusing on activities you enjoy

- Focusing too little on assigned activities

- Having difficulty with organization

- Interrupting others

- Blurting out an idea because you're afraid that if you don't say it right away you'll forget it

- Having difficulty with coordination; clumsiness

- Tending to "overdo"

- Feeling like you don't fit in socially

- Feeling like everyone else knows some social rules that you don't know

Positives of ADD

There are many positives to having ADD. Studies have shown that people with ADD can be more creative than non-ADD people, although they have difficulties with practicality (Abraham et al. 2006). People with ADD are versatile and can switch easily from task to task. They generally have a good sense of humor and are quick witted. People with ADD can have a strong sense of justice and be very active and effective when involved in social causes. All of these are positive characteristics to take with you to college. And the best part is that they are already built in!

Causes of ADD

You may have heard people say that ADD doesn't exist, that it is really just laziness or a result of watching too much television. You may have even had people tell you that if you had been disciplined more as a child you wouldn't have these problems. These statements are simply not true. People with ADD have differences in brain structure. The size of the ADD brain's cerebellar lobes is different from that of people without ADD (Mackie et al. 2007). ADD is also highly genetic, with a heritability rate of 75 percent (Rietveld et al. 2004). This means that there is a 75 percent chance that your ADD is caused by genetics.

ADD affects the frontal lobes of the brain. These lobes are responsible for the *executive functions*, performing tasks like those of a corporate executive—transmitting information, planning ahead, learning from errors, keeping emotions at an even keel, determining the length of time for a task, creating motivation, and knowing the appropriate thing to say. When you have ADD, impairment in these areas can result in difficulty retaining information, lateness for appointments, repetition of the same mistakes, mood swings, difficulty understanding social cues or rules, and difficulty making yourself follow through with tasks.

In high school, your parents may have motivated you through positive encouragement and negative consequences. Now it is up to you to motivate yourself. One of the issues of ADD is that it's not so much a problem with attention, but a problem with motivation. It is difficult for your brain to motivate itself to start or stop a task. That explains why it is difficult for you to focus on reading an assigned book but so easy for you to hyperfocus on playing video games. Once your brain gets motivated, it is really motivated; it can be difficult for you to quit something once you are on a roll.

YOUR NEW LIFE

You may have "helicopter parents," who hover over you even when you're away at college. You may get more phone calls, e-mail, or visits than you feel are necessary. While everyone has their parents involved in their education to some extent, people with ADD are more likely to have parent intervention. Mom and Dad have been monitoring the completion of your homework and school projects since you were little. They may even have had to bail you out of sticky situations, and they have spent a great many years supporting you, encouraging you, and creating structure for you. Naturally, it can be difficult for parents to let go when they have devoted a large part of their lives to ensuring your success. Be patient. They'll gradually find reason to relax a bit. (Tip: the better you're doing in college, the less hovering will occur.)

However, don't be afraid to ask your parents for help and support—most students have challenges in college, whether they have ADD or not. Don't fall into the trap of thinking that you have to handle everything yourself, on your own. When you realize you need support, it's a sign of strength, not weakness. Your parents will always be your parents no matter how old you are.

The biggest difference between college and high school is that you are much more independent than you were before—you are now totally responsible for yourself. You are the CEO of your life now. Up to now, your parents may have watched you like a hawk to make sure you were doing your homework. That's a thing of the past. You are now in charge of completing all your course work without any prompting or prodding. If your mom or dad woke you up in the morning, you will now need to learn how to get up, on time, on your own. (It can be quite a shock when you forget to set your alarm clock and wake up late the day of a test.)

You may engage in behaviors or activities that would not be permissible at home. But that doesn't mean you'll avoid the consequences of those behaviors. If you stay up too late or use alcohol or drugs, you may be too tired to stay awake in class, or you may not study enough and bomb a test.

You are now in charge of your finances. You decide how much you will pay for something, whether you really need to buy that item, and what to do when you don't have enough money for something (this is where the "Dear Mom and Dad, I need money" e-mail comes in). Many students also have to contend with paperwork for the first time. Mom and Dad may have completed forms for you when you were in high school, but now it's up to you to know which forms and deadlines the college requires of you. Luckily, today most colleges have forms, rules, and academic calendars available online, making it easier for you to navigate those bureaucratic seas.

Your friends may give you tips and suggestions intended to help you. Indeed, many people with ADD feel that they cannot make good decisions, or that they cannot trust their judgment because of past difficulties. Just remember that you are the authority on you. You are a capable, intelligent, and successful student. And one of the nice things about college is that, regardless of your past performance, you can use it as an opportunity to start over.

I moved from Seattle to Boston. It's a lot of responsibility all at once. It's like, "Welcome to Adulthood!" There's all these things you never had to think about before, and all of a sudden you are the one responsible for your life and your future.
—Amy, freshman, Berklee College of Music

FINDING THE RIGHT COLLEGE FOR YOU

You'll handle your new independence better if you've chosen the right environment for your college experience. Which would be more comfortable for you: being a big fish in a small pond or a small fish in a big pond? Would you prefer to be recognized on campus, or would you rather be anonymous? The size of campus you need largely depends on where you grew up, your personality, and your comfort level. If you are from a small, rural area with twenty-five people in your graduating class, moving to a large campus may be quite a shock. Some people, however, want the new experience of being around a lot of students. In large schools, it is up to you to make yourself known to others on campus. If you are from a large city and are used to anonymity, you may feel more at home on a large campus than you would at a small school.

To help you identify possible schools to check out, use the online "college wizards" and "college finders," which can help you narrow your choices of colleges based on campus size, location, major, and even SAT scores and GPA. (Website addresses for these services can be found in the Resources section at the end of this book.) You might also consider talking to your high school's college counselor, or hiring a professional consultant, to help with this process.

Visit the colleges you're considering. During your visit, attend some classes and talk with current students. You may also be able to take a tour of the residence halls. If your college offers an overnight tour, definitely attend it. You may be able to stay in the residence halls and try out what it would be like to go to school there. When you're visiting a particular campus, you may get a strong feeling that this is where you want to go to school. Trust that intuition.

Next, let's take a closer look at some of the issues to consider when you're deciding which colleges to apply to.

Both rational and nonrational factors contributed to my choosing Vanderbilt for college. I was offered some financial grants and enticed by the opportunity to indulge my enjoyment of music by living in Music City, USA. But I was primarily drawn to Vanderbilt because I saw it as the institution where I could best transition myself from being a high school student to a college student. Going there just felt right.

—Jonathan, senior, Vanderbilt University

Class Size

People with ADD benefit greatly from a smaller class size because it often results in more individualized attention. On large campuses, you may attend some classes where there are three hundred students or more. Find out the college's ratio of students to teachers by contacting their admissions department or visiting their website. You may also be able to attend some classes during your visit to the campus. Contact the college's visitors' center for more information.

Distance from Home

You may also want to consider how far away you want to be from home. If you have a close-knit family, you may feel more comfortable going to school within driving distance of your family. But be aware that if you go home every weekend to visit friends or family you will be missing out on the college experience. Being away from campus also disrupts your study time.

I keep in contact with my family through my phone and my computer. Because cell phones now have nationwide long-distance calling at the same price as local calling, keeping in touch with family members is much easier and cheaper. I can talk to my family several times a day if I choose and it will not cost me anything but the minutes that I already pay for my monthly cell phone bill. Also, I speak to many family and friends using instant messaging and e-mail. Since I am on my computer for a lot of the day, it is a convenient way for me to converse with family and friends. An advantage of using the computer to communicate is that we can use our webcams to see and talk to each other, send pictures, and share videos that we have. The Internet and the cell phone really have broken the long-distance barrier.

—Ayal, senior, UCLA

Cost of College

A major deciding factor for you will likely be the cost of tuition. You may be getting student loans, or your parents may be footing the bill. Either way, it is important to remember that a more expensive school does not necessarily equal a better education. Colleges geared toward students with ADD may be a great option, but keep in mind that they are almost exclusively private schools and therefore cost more.

Before you shell out the big bucks, talk to students who have attended the college and find out their opinions about whether it's a cost-effective school. And be sure to look carefully at the types of financial aid and scholarships colleges offer.

TYPES OF FINANCIAL AID

There are four types of funding available for college students: grants, loans, work-study, and scholarships. You can apply for these funds in any year of college by filling out a financial aid application. Students in the United States seeking financial aid are required to fill out a Free Application for Federal Student Aid (FAFSA) form, either online or on paper. You'll need your parents' help to fill out and sign the FAFSA form if you are a dependent (in other words, if you are under the age of twenty-five and your parents still claim you as a dependent on their tax return forms). There is no fee to process your application. See the Resources section at the end of this book for FAFSA contact information.

Since people with ADD usually have at least one ADD parent, and people with ADD are not good at details, double-check all of your loan paperwork before sending it in. Make sure the FAFSA form is signed. Just to be safe, ask a staff member in the financial aid office if he or she will review the form before you send it in. An error in your paperwork can cost you precious time (and money).

Even if you don't think you're eligible for financial aid, it can't hurt to just send in the form. In 2005, 1.5 million undergraduates didn't submit a FAFSA form even though they were eligible for Pell Grants (American Council on Education 2006).

The amount you receive in financial aid is determined by the cost of your college, including (but not limited to) tuition, books, and room and board; your family's expected contribution (determined by income and benefits); and your financial need. This *financial aid package* is a combination of various types of funding presented to you by the college's financial aid office. If you are deciding between two different colleges, each college may offer you a financial aid package that differs in the amount of funding, including the amount of loans and your family's expected contribution.

If you feel that the aid offered does not meet your financial needs, you had a change in financial circumstances (such as a parent being laid off), or you left out important information on your application (which might have affected the amount of aid awarded to you), visit or call the college's financial aid office to request an appeal. Be prepared to provide documentation of the reason for your appeal. In addition, keep in mind that some colleges may ask to see your competing offers of financial aid.

Grants. Grants are monetary awards that you do not have to pay back. They are awarded by private organizations, professional associations, educational institutions, state governments, and the federal government. U.S. Federal Pell Grants are need-based funds for undergraduates with low income. If you qualify for a Pell Grant, you have the opportunity to receive two other grants: the Academic Competitiveness (AC) Grant and the National Science and Mathematics Access to Retain Talent (SMART) Grant. The AC Grant is for students who have completed rigorous academic high-school programs, including the International Baccalaureate program or Advanced Placement classes. The SMART Grant is for college students in their junior or senior year who are majoring in science, engineering, or a foreign language that is deemed critical to national security. The website addresses for these grants can be found in the Resources section at the end of this book.

Loans. The key feature of a student loan is that you must pay it back, plus interest, after you graduate from college. Borrow only what you need, because you will eventually need to pay it all back. People with ADD often overestimate how much money they will earn in the future and minimize the impact of loan repayments, so make sure you're realistic about how much you'll be able to repay.

Stafford loans are awarded to students by the U.S. Department of Education. They are offered in two forms—subsidized or unsubsidized. Subsidized Stafford loans are based on financial need, while unsubsidized loans are not. With a subsidized loan, you will not accrue any interest while you are in school. With an unsubsidized loan, you will accrue interest while you are in school, although at a low rate. Keep in mind that if you take out $2,000 in an unsubsidized loan at 6 percent, paid over ten years, you are really borrowing a total of $2,664.

Loan forgiveness programs, in which people work in return for full or partial forgiveness of their loans, are available for people in some types of professions, such as teachers and other service providers, usually in underserved regions. In chapter 10, you'll learn more about the loan payback process. To find information on loan forgiveness programs, see the Resources section at the end of this book.

Work-study. Work-study jobs are employment opportunities on campus, assigned based on financial need. If you have a work-study job, you can work a maximum of twenty hours a week, and you get paid at an hourly rate. Work-study jobs can provide you with great experiences for your future career. You will meet people in academia, and they may be able to provide you with recommendation letters when you start your job search or graduate school application process.

If you are interested in a work-study position, check the box next to "work-study" on your FAFSA form. If you qualify for a work-study job, you may get an e-mail or letter from the college notifying you of a work-study workshop on campus. Available work-study positions may be posted at your college's financial aid office or website.

Scholarships. Scholarships are awards or gifts of money that are given based on need, achievement, cultural background, or disability; unlike loans, they do not need to be repaid. Scholarships can be paid directly to you, or directly to the university. There are some scholarships available for people with ADD and/or learning disabilities. In addition, many large companies and unions fund scholarships for the children (and sometimes even the grandchildren) of their employees. In some states, housing costs may be covered for students who receive an in-state scholarship based on their GPA (see your state's Department of Education for details).

Start researching and applying for scholarships during your junior year of high school. You do have the option to hire a company to research scholarship information for you, for a fee. However, if you have Internet access, you can do this search on your own and save money. See the Resources section at the end of this book for websites that can help you find information on scholarships.

> I decided on NC State because it was in-state tuition and a good school. I didn't want to pay out-of-state tuition someplace else and get the same education. That just doesn't make sense.
> —Mike, senior, North Carolina State

Types of Colleges

Not all colleges are alike. As you look at colleges, you'll find that most fall into one of the following categories: two year or four year; state or private; and religious or secular. In addition, the atmosphere in some private schools can range from intensely competitive to relaxed and nontraditional. You might consider starting at a two-year community college and then transferring to a four-year school to finish your degree. Depending on the quality of the school, a community college can sometimes offer people with ADD smaller class size, lower fees, less pressure, and more personalized attention from staff who assist students with disabilities.

Some colleges are affiliated with a religious group, while some are secular (no religious affiliation). If your religious upbringing is an important part of your life, you might want to consider attending a college where students have similar values.

College Information Worksheet

When you are looking at a particular college, consult the admissions office, current students, alumni, periodicals that review colleges, and websites to research the answers to the following questions.

- What is the student-to-teacher ratio?

- How far away is the campus from home?

- Does the college offer enough spaces in required classes for the number of students in the school?

- What is the cost of the college?

- What is the distance from the residence halls to the classrooms?

- What is the reputation of their Office of Student Disabilities?

- Does the college offer the major I am interested in?

- How does the college rank in my field of study?

- What percentage of the classes are taught by professors, and what percentage are taught by graduate students?

- What percentage of students graduate?

- What percentage of students find employment immediately after graduation?

Support Services

You may be interested in seeking special accommodations due to your ADD while you're in college. Accommodations include permission to have extended time on tests and a reduced course load. It is important that you learn about the services available through the college's Office of Student Disability Services (OSDS) before you apply to that school. (You will apply for those services after you select your college.) You can find out specific information about accommodations in chapter 5.

Although the federal laws state that colleges that receive federal funding must provide "reasonable accommodations" for students with ADD, the scope of those services changes from campus to campus. You can find out more information about a college's student services from the school's website, course catalog, admissions information packet, orientation paperwork, or student handbook. You can also call the university and ask to talk with the OSDS directly.

When you contact the OSDS, you may find it helpful to ask the following questions:

- How many students with ADD do you serve?

- Is there a support group available for students with ADD?

- Do you have a list of ADD specialists in the area?

- When I visit the campus, can I meet with an ADD student who uses your services?

- Does a member of your staff help with orientation?

- Do you have an on-call number?

- Is there a physician at the student health care center who has experience treating people with ADD and prescribes medication for it?

- What specific accommodations do you suggest for a student with ADD?

Narrowing Your Choices

Making decisions can be difficult for people with ADD. Once you have found some colleges you like, fill out the following worksheet for each college to help decide which ones to apply to.

College name: _____

My first impression of this college: _____

ADD Services: (Circle all that apply.)

      Support group   Specialized staff   On-call staff

Tuition per year: _____

Distance from home: _____

Scholarship or other monies available: _____

Is on-campus housing available? _____

      Cost per semester: _____

Size of campus: _____ students

Does the school offer my major? _____

APPLYING FOR COLLEGE ADMISSION

Once you have narrowed down your list of colleges you want to attend, it's time to start adding the application deadlines to your calendar, making lists of all the required paperwork, filling out applications, and gathering letters of recommendation. It's generally a good idea to apply to at least six colleges: two highly selective institutions, two where acceptance is more likely, and two colleges where you are virtually guaranteed to be accepted.

The application process involves planning ahead and attention to detail, so you (like many students with and without ADD) may wish to ask for guidance and help from an organized, supportive family member or teacher.

Early Admission Applications

As you travel through the exciting world of college applications, you may hear about "early admissions." As you might expect, this type of application gives you earlier acceptance results. There are two types of early admission programs: early action and early decision. Both have application deadlines and notification of admission decisions that are earlier than those of the regular admissions process. Early action admissions do not require you to commit to that particular college if you are accepted—you can still apply to other colleges and compare financial aid offers. However, early decision admissions require that you promise to attend if you are accepted to that school. If you are accepted as an early decision applicant, you must withdraw your applications at all other colleges. Obviously, you will have many more options available to you if you go with the early action admissions process over the early decision admissions process.

Your College Application Timeline

For the average student, applying to college may resemble the experience of having been dropped off in the middle of nowhere without a map or compass. If you have ADD, you may feel like you've been dropped off in the middle of nowhere without a map or compass, *and* it's 110 degrees out. It can be a little overwhelming. Here's a timeline that will let you know when certain tasks need to be completed during your senior year.

September

☐ Review your grades and test scores with your guidance counselor.

☐ Make a list of the colleges you'd most like to attend.

- ☐ If you would like to receive special accommodations for ADD, contact each college's Office of Student Disability Services to see what services they offer to ADD students and what forms are required.
- ☐ Obtain admission applications for these schools (get more than one, or make photocopies of the blank application in case you make an error) or start viewing them online.
- ☐ Write the application deadlines in your calendar or planner.
- ☐ Assemble a list of people to ask for recommendation letters, such as your employer, your favorite high-school teacher, and a highly respected family friend.

October

- ☐ Ask for recommendation letters.
- ☐ Start filling out college applications.
- ☐ Write application essays and have them reviewed for grammatical or content issues.
- ☐ Complete and submit "early admission" applications.
- ☐ Take the SAT or ACT again if it might help improve your scores (some colleges take the average of your scores).
- ☐ Start researching financial aid and scholarships.

November

- ☐ Write scholarship application deadlines in your planner or calendar.
- ☐ Submit college applications.

December

- ☐ Continue researching scholarships.
- ☐ Send thank-you notes to people who have written recommendation letters for you.

January

- ☐ Complete and submit the Free Application for Federal Student Aid (FAFSA) by mail or online starting January 1 if you are interested in receiving financial assistance.

February and March

- ☐ If a college has not notified you that they received your application, call them to confirm they did receive it.

April

- ☐ Receive acceptance or decline notices from colleges.
- ☐ Visit colleges where you have been accepted.
- ☐ Review financial aid packages and appeal, if necessary.

May

- ☐ Make your final decision about which college you want to attend.
- ☐ Send in any required paperwork and deposits to the college of your choice, including any forms or documents required by the Office of Student Disability Services (if you are seeking accommodations).
- ☐ Rest and relax!

Dealing with Disappointment

It's normal to be upset when you find out you didn't get accepted to a college—it can feel like a personal rejection. However, being denied admission has nothing to do with you personally, nor is it a measure of your ability to succeed in the future. The college you applied to may have had an unusually large amount of applicants that semester, or they may only have a specific number of spaces available in a degree program. Since you may be a tad on the impulsive side, make sure you read the rejection letter all the way through. You may find that you have been placed on a waiting list instead.

Let's say you find out you haven't been accepted to any colleges. This is rare, but it does happen. Look into attending a community college for your first two years of schooling, and then transfer to a four-year school. You may find that the smaller average class size at a community college works to your advantage. You can also apply to schools whose deadlines haven't passed. If you are determined to get accepted at one of the colleges to which you originally applied, determine the reason for the initial rejection letter, and check to see if there's a process for reapplying to the college. Rarely, students have appealed a rejection letter and the college has reversed its decision.

Choosing and getting into a good college is important, but more important is what you make of your time there. At least some of your time, especially at first, will be spent figuring out how to address the practical challenges of being in college. One of the biggest challenges is that you might be sharing a room for the first time in your life—and possibly sharing it with a total stranger!

In this chapter you learned about the symptoms of ADD, how ADD can affect your college experience, and how to find a college that best suits your needs. In the next chapter, you will learn about finding a place to live, sharing living quarters with your roommate(s), what to bring to college, and how to get around once you're there.

Home Away from Home

Living on your own, especially when you first move away from home, can be an exciting, scary, frustrating, and fun experience. In this chapter, you will learn about housing options, how to find roommates, and how to get along with your roommates (especially if you have a tendency toward messiness). You will also learn how to determine the best methods of transportation while you are at school.

OH, GIVE ME A HOME . . .

You have the option to live either on campus or off during your college experience. As is the case with most choices in life, there are advantages and disadvantages to each. It's all about what works best for you.

On-Campus Housing

If you choose to live on campus, you'll be living in a residence hall, or "dorm." Residence halls have evolved into full-service complexes that have laundry facilities, restaurants, and even convenience stores. Some residence halls still have "barracks-style" floor plans, where one hundred residents are housed per floor, with two residents per room. These residence halls usually have a community bathroom and shared kitchen area. However, a newer trend in residence halls is the apartment-style floor plan, where four residents live together in a suite, each with his or her own bedroom and a shared bathroom. Residence-hall amenities depend on the college and how much you are willing to pay. Check with the college's housing office for more information.

ADVANTAGES

- Living in a residence hall is less expensive than living in an apartment.

- Rooms are furnished.

- Residence halls are located within walking distance of classes.

- Utilities (electricity, telephone, Internet) are included in rent.

- You pay only one fee per semester rather than paying rent every month.

- It's easier to get involved in campus activities when living in residence halls.

- A resident assistant lives on each floor to assist with any concerns.

DISADVANTAGES

- Residence hall rooms tend to be smaller than apartments.

- You may have to share a room.

- You may have to share bathroom facilities.

- You'll have less freedom and more restrictions in a residence hall than you would in an apartment.

One definite benefit of living on campus is that you'll have a mentor and helper living on your floor—this person is called a resident assistant (RA). At most schools, an RA has been a student at the university for at least a year and has special training in helping residents. You can go to your RA if you have any questions or concerns. After you've attended the school for a year or more, you might want to consider becoming an RA yourself. At many colleges, RAs live on campus at a reduced rate, get paid for their services, and, most important, they have a positive impact on the lives of the residents.

Off-Campus Housing

Students often find off-campus housing at apartment complexes. Apartments can have one to four bedrooms; studios (one- or two-room apartments with combination bedroom and living room) are also available in many places. Depending on how many roommates you have, you may have your own bedroom and bathroom, or you may share. In many cases, you'll be asked to sign a lease, usually for a year, and you pay a monthly rental fee. Utilities are usually not included in the rent. In some cases, students rent houses with a few other students, or they may rent a room in an established household.

ADVANTAGES

- You'll have more independence and freedom than you would in a residence hall.

- Off-campus housing may offer more privacy and a quieter living environment than a residence hall would.

- You may have larger living quarters than you would in a residence hall.

- You may have more amenities in an apartment or home than a residence hall would offer.

DISADVANTAGES

- Off-campus apartments and homes are often more expensive than residence halls.

- You'll have more bills to pay than you would if you were living in a residence hall.

- You may have a longer commute to campus.

- You'll have to provide your own furniture, unless you rent a furnished apartment.

You may have more independence and freedom when you live off campus, but this has its own drawbacks. Going from following your parents' rules to living with no rules at all can be overwhelming. If you already have issues with impulse control, living on campus can give you some needed structure, particularly during your first year of college.

On Campus or Off Campus?

To help determine which living situation would best suit you, place a check mark next to the three items that are most important to you:

☐ A. Living near my classes

☐ B. Becoming more familiar with campus and college life

☐ C. Having the freedom to make my own rules

☐ D. Saving money on rent

☐ E. Having a larger living space

☐ F. Having more privacy and quiet

If the three items you chose were A, B, and D, you may benefit more from living on campus. If you chose C, E, and F, you may find that living off campus suits your needs. Regardless of the items you chose, if this is your first year in college, you may want to strongly consider living on campus anyway. This would give you a chance to really focus on college life and your course work as you get accustomed to living away from home. In addition, your college may actually offer housing options that are similar to those found off campus, such as apartment-style residence halls. Remember, you can always live off campus next year.

WHOM WILL YOU LIVE WITH?

Once you've figured out whether you'll be living on or off campus, you'll need to decide what your living situation will look like: at home with Mom and Dad, with a roommate, or by yourself? Let's look at your choices, below.

Living at Home

Plenty of students commute to school while staying with their parents—a living situation that has its own set of advantages and disadvantages. Living at home can really cut costs and make it easier to save money. This is also a helpful situation if you have close family ties—you eliminate the homesickness that a lot of college students experience. It can also make the transition to college much easier. On the other hand, if your family tends to have a lot of conflict or if there are several members of your family living in the home, you may prefer to live elsewhere.

Living in a Co-op

A co-op is a form of housing where you live with roommates and do household chores (usually a set number of hours a week) in return for reduced housing costs. You can find co-ops where residents share similar majors, such as a co-op for communication majors or health care majors. For more information, see the Resources section at the end of this book.

Living by Yourself

Although it may be more expensive, living on your own can mean decreased distractions, less noise, and fewer interruptions. Living alone also eliminates the possibility of conflict with roommates because, well, you won't have any. However, you may wind up feeling more isolated, which may make it difficult for you to stay motivated. If you want the privacy and quiet of living alone but also want to be close to your classes, campus activities, the library, and your peers, check with your college's housing office about the availability of single residence-hall rooms.

Living with Roommates

Roommates are interesting creatures. Although most roommates are happy with just food, water, and a place to live, others may require more maintenance and a larger apartment. In this section, you will learn how to choose and live with a roommate who fits your lifestyle.

Having a roommate reduces your costs and provides social interaction. Living alone works for some people, but people with ADD generally need people around in order to avoid feeling isolated. But how do you find someone you can get along with? You can either find a friend ahead of time or play "roommate roulette." If you live on campus, the college's housing office can randomly assign you a roommate. If you are living off campus, you may be able to find an apartment complex or service that offers "roommate matching" based on your age, major, and preferences. There are costs and benefits associated with both living situations.

LIVING WITH FRIENDS

You may have a friend or even a relative who will be attending the same school as you and has agreed to be your roommate. (If you'll be staying in a residence hall, check with the school's housing office to see if you can request a particular roommate, since policies vary.) The upside is that you already know his personality, and you are probably also aware of his quirks, like his need to brush his teeth after every meal. There is also an increased level of trust when you live with someone you already know—you are less likely to worry about your stuff disappearing. Similarly, your roommate will probably already be aware of your tendency toward disorganization and may have a greater appreciation of your positive qualities, like your warped sense of humor. In addition, you can get together with your roommate ahead of time and plan who is going to bring what, and you can also pick out your décor together.

However, knowing your roommate beforehand can lead to some sticky situations. You most likely did not live in close quarters with your friend or relative before. You may find things out about your roommate that you weren't privy to—like the fact that he compulsively flosses his teeth and then leaves the floss on his desk. You may also find that living away from home for the first time can bring about changes in your roommate's personality. Your formerly quiet best friend suddenly stays out partying until four in the morning every night. As you might guess, although knowing your roommate ahead of time can cut down on certain stressors, it can also permanently change your relationship.

LIVING WITH STRANGERS: PLAYING "ROOMMATE ROULETTE"

You may have a roommate selected for you through the college's housing office, or you may sign up for a service that matches you up with apartment roommates. Some colleges tell you the name and contact number of your roommate ahead of time, while others don't let you know who your roommate is until you show up at school. Playing "roommate roulette" has lots of pros and cons. On the plus side, you get to know a new person—one with whom you may form a lasting friendship. In addition, nothing teaches you flexibility and adaptation like sharing a 10-by-10-foot room with a total stranger. If you can learn to do that, you can do anything.

Some unique challenges can arise, however. You may find that the only thing you and your roommate have in common is that you're both carbon-based life-forms. You may have radically different moral or political views. You may also have different tastes in décor—you want to decorate the room with pictures of fluffy kittens, while your roommate wants to put up photos of dead flowers. However, keep in mind that if you and your roommate are very different it can offer a wonderful opportunity for you to learn how to get along with others. Diversity is what makes life interesting.

Roommate Questionnaire

When interviewing a potential roommate, find out the answers to the following questions:

Morning person or night owl? _____

Drinks alcohol? _____ How much, and how often? _____

Smokes? _____

Favorite music _____

Favorite free-time activities _____

Messy or neat? _____

Lived with roommates before? _____

Major _____

Year in school _____

Works outside of school? _____ Hours? _____

Significant other? _____

See how much your potential roommate's answers mesh with your own. The more answers that match, the more potential the person has for being your roommate.

_____

GETTING ALONG

In a perfect world, your roommates would always pay their rent on time, they would be totally okay with a messy apartment, they would be quiet when you needed them to be quiet, and they wouldn't bring any furry creatures into the apartment. Alas, this is not a perfect world, and you may encounter some of these challenges. In this section, you will learn how to cope effectively with your roommates with regard to a variety of common issues.

Rent issues. One of the issues roommates living off campus face is when one of the roommates cannot or will not pay their rent on time. This can result in late fees for everyone and, in extreme cases, even get you evicted from the apartment. If you and your roommate are on the same rental contract, you could be responsible for paying that person's rent. A simple solution is to find an apartment complex that will draw up separate rental contracts for you and your roommates. If a roommate skips out on rent, your occupancy of the apartment is not affected. Before you sign any contract you'll need to be clear on whether you are responsible for finding a new roommate when someone moves out.

Disagreements. Disagreements are a normal part of life, but life can become quite uncomfortable if you and your roommate have a disagreement. People with ADD can be prone to mood swings and can get frustrated easily. In addition, they are not always aware of the impact their behavior has on others. If this is true for you, you may also have difficulty with social skills, so you may feel intimidated or unprepared when talking to your roommate about an issue. For more information on successfully working out conflicts with others, see chapter 9.

Messiness. If you have ADD, you are more likely to be on the messy side of the organizational spectrum. Having a roommate with a tendency toward tidiness can work two ways: Your roommate can become an "organization coach" and show you how to get your things in order, or at least be a good role model for neatness. Or, your roommate may complain and criticize your messiness without providing any helpful feedback. Either way, you are equally responsible for maintaining cleanliness in the common living areas, such as the kitchen and living room. With any luck, your roommate won't even care that you're organizationally challenged. He or she may just want your shoes off the kitchen counter!

If you're living in an apartment or house, try to at least keep the common living areas clean. If you have your own room, you can keep it at whatever level of order or disorder you want, but make sure you pick up after yourself in rooms that everyone uses. Take fifteen minutes at the end of each day to go around and collect your stuff from different rooms of your apartment. If you're sharing a residence hall room, it's a good idea to keep your side of the room reasonably neat at all times (even if your roommate is messier than you are!). Here are a few ways to keep the mess from getting out of hand: try to make your bed regularly, put your dirty laundry in the hamper, empty the garbage frequently, and never let food sit around for more than a few minutes.

Schedule and noise conflicts. What if your roommate is a night owl and you're a morning person? He might stay up late listening to the stereo while you need to get some sleep. First, talk to your roommate. Use "I feel" language, and mention how you propose to resolve the issue. For example, "When you play your death metal music late at night, I feel frustrated because I have a difficult time sleeping. Would you mind turning it down after ten o'clock?" Make sure you don't use any value judgments, such as, "Hey loser, your music is too loud!"

It's amazing how many conflicts start because people are hesitant to talk to others about how their behavior affects them. Just bringing it out in the open can help. In chapter 9, you will learn effective ways of communicating your concerns. If talking to your roommate doesn't help, invest in some earplugs and an eye mask. If that doesn't work, you might want to consider whether it's worth it to talk with your RA, if you're living in the residence hall, or find other living accommodations.

The most invaluable items I brought to school with me were earplugs.
—Lori, senior, University of Minnesota

Pets and college. Generally, it is best to avoid having a pet while in college. Yes, pets can help reduce stress and they can be fun to have around. However, they can also lead to increased expenses and roommate squabbles, and they require consistent care. Many residence halls and apartments have rules about what animals are allowed, if any—in fact, you can be fined if it is discovered that you are harboring a pet. In addition, you'll need to figure out what to do with your pet when you go home for vacations; attesting to this common problem is the epidemic of abandoned pets that routinely turn up at the end of each school year.

Allergies are another complication when pets are involved. If you are allergic to animals, you'll need to tell your roommate right away. This is a serious health issue, and you should treat it as such. If your roommate says, "Oh, I'll keep my hamster/cat/dog/ferret in my room, so it won't be a problem," this is not acceptable. You can still have an asthma or allergy attack. See if you can develop a no-pets policy that you both agree to from the beginning.

To disclose or not to disclose. You might want to consider telling your roommate about your ADD. Or you may just want to say that you tend to be on the messy and disorganized side—it's better to warn someone ahead of time rather than have him be surprised when he comes in and can't see the floor of your room.

Before you disclose to your roommate that you have ADD, ask yourself about your level of trust in that person. Once you tell your roommate that you have ADD, you can't really stop him from telling other people. So only share this information if you are very sure that it will be kept in confidence. Definitely refrain from saying anything if you're concerned that your roommate would try to get access to your medication.

> I've really found ADD to be hidden blessing. Knowing that I've always had it, but finally giving a name to it, gives those around me better tools to handle my quirks.
>
> —Cheryl, junior, University of Calgary

Know your rights. It's important to remember that even if you have ADD and are messy, you have the same basic rights as everyone else. And since people with ADD often feel a need to please others, they may forgo their rights in order to keep others happy. However, when you do this, you are doing yourself a big disservice. You have:

- The right to feel safe in your residence

- The right to have guests if they behave respectfully

- The right to be free from being teased or harassed

- The right to have your belongings to yourself and only used by others with your permission

- The right to change your mind

- The right to a healthy atmosphere, including clean air and a low level of noise

- The right to practice your belief system without harassment

If you feel that your rights have been violated, first talk with your roommates. See chapter 9 for an effective method for resolving conflict. If necessary, talk with your RA (if you have one). As a last resort, consider moving to another apartment or room. Speak to the apartment management or housing office about other housing options.

EVERYTHING BUT THE KITCHEN SINK: PACKING FOR COLLEGE

While you're in college, you want to keep your living space as low maintenance as possible. So bring a bare minimum of items—less stuff means less potential mess.

You can always buy items once you get to college. But be careful not to join the stampede that occurs at retail stores the week before classes start. A good guideline is to only bring enough stuff to fill up the trunk and backseat of a medium-size car. Bringing what you need instead of buying it when you get there is less expensive, and it gives you time to focus on meeting new people and getting to know the campus, instead of shopping.

Think Vertical

When figuring out storage options, think vertical. You have a lot more vertical space than horizontal space. Find organizational items that stack—cubes, for example. You can get attractive organization products at reasonable prices—crates, bins, binders, and folders. It can be helpful to have nice-looking organization containers, since it gives you more motivation to keep your area neat, and stackable crates and the like will allow you to have more free space. Websites that sell organizational products are listed in the Resources section at the end of this book.

Think Small

If you'll be living in a residence hall, bring smaller versions of items. You probably don't need the industrial-size shampoo and conditioner. They take up a lot of space, even when they are only half full. Smaller sizes may cost more per ounce, but they'll save you space and time. It's not worth rearranging your closet just to fit a couple of large bottles in. You can also bring smaller versions of appliances, such as mini microwaves and refrigerators. However, check before you arrive on campus to see if your new residence has these appliances in a common area. You'll find it more efficient both in cost and space to use a community microwave.

Think Safe

You'll need to take special care to maintain safety in your new home. Never burn candles or incense, since people with ADD are more prone to forget to extinguish them. Similarly, use appliances that have automatic shut-off features, so you won't have to dash back to your room in the middle of a class when you suddenly realize you may have forgotten to unplug something. Be sure to read the apartment complex or residence hall policies to find out what is allowed and not allowed in your apartment or room.

Think Labeling

Get a small portable labeling machine and some permanent markers and put your name on everything. You'll be surprised at how many identical backpacks are brought to college. Information on labeling machines can be found in the Resources section at the end of this book.

Think Ahead

If you're in touch with your roommate ahead of time, talk about what items each of you is bringing to college. Do you really need two toasters? You can also coordinate your décor with your roommate ahead of time. If you don't know your roommate before you arrive on campus, it's possible that you will both show up with the same appliances. If this happens, decide whose toaster or microwave you'll keep in the room, and send the duplicate home with the other person's family.

Think Visual

Consider purchasing a dry-erase board and markers. (Make sure the markers say "dry erase" on them. It's difficult to remove permanent marker from a dry-erase board.) This way, you can jot down notes or ideas that pop into your head without having to write them on little bits of paper that would eventually get lost. If you put it right inside the front door, you can write down those thoughts that pop into your mind as you are returning home, and you can make notes to yourself about things you need to remember.

Think Ergonomic

Since you'll be taking your books, notebooks, and school supplies to class, you need an easy and ergonomic way to carry your stuff. You want a bag that distributes weight equally across your back. You may see students with their backpacks hanging off their shoulder by one strap. Although that may look cool, it can cause back strain. Always use both straps when wearing your backpack. A sturdy, good-looking bag doesn't have to be expensive. Of course, what you put in your backpack is just as important; we will talk about that in chapter 3.

Think Organized

You will need a way to keep track of your assignments and social plans. You have two options: a paper planner, or a digital organizer.

Paper planners are your standard calendars and schedulers. Some colleges even give them out for free at the beginning of the semester, and these are handy because they usually list the college's events and deadlines. If you can't get a free one, planners are still relatively inexpensive to buy. They are easy to use, and some allow you to add extra pages. Make sure you occasionally photocopy or scan your planner pages—that way, if you lose your planner, at least you'll have a backup.

Planners can get bulky and may look messy, especially if you have a couple hundred little yellow notes sticking out of it. At the same time, it can be useful to paperclip or stick notes to the pages in your planner, and that's tough to do with a digital organizer. Of course, digital organizers have plenty of positive aspects. Yes, they are more expensive than paper planners, but you have the added security of being able to back it up onto your computer. Changes to your schedule look neater and you won't have to deal with erasing or crossing through items, as you do with a paper planner. If you have difficulty writing neatly (as many people with ADD do), digital organizers make it much easier for you to read what you've written. You can also look into getting an all-in-one device that contains your calendar, to-do list, telephone, MP3 player, and various programs, such as word processing or Internet service.

Digital organizers are much smaller than paper planners, and this can be both a blessing and a curse. It is easy to take your digital organizer with you—you can just put it in your pocket or purse. However, the small size also means it's more likely to get lost. If you are offered equipment protection insurance on your digital organizer, get it. The insurance usually covers incidents of loss or damage resulting from your digital organizer taking a swim in your bathroom sink.

> I keep a large desk calendar in my car. Visually, it is the best way to go, because the calendar yells at you. You can just look over at it and see where you are supposed to be going. But a smaller planner is better for social graces.
> —Jason, sophomore, Hillsborough Community College

Electronics

Ah, where would we be without our gadgets? For many, bringing the right electronics to school is as important as (if not more than) bringing the right clothes. Make sure you have packed the following in your arsenal:

- Cell phone (with charger)

- Camera (with charger)

- MP3 player, with headphones or earbuds

- Backup batteries for each item

- Computer

- External hard drive (to run scheduled automatic backups)

- Power strip with surge protection and circuit breaker

Many colleges require their students to have a laptop computer with a certain amount of memory, speed, and software. Check with your college for specifications. Some computer manufacturers and software makers have special rates for students.

In addition to getting an external hard drive, consider using a data storage website. Some of them provide 5 GB of storage at a low monthly charge or for free. See the Resources section for more details.

Clothing

Take a good look at your clothing before you haul it to college. Do you really need to take five pairs of jeans to college? College residence halls *do* have washing machines. Take three pairs of jeans maximum. If you haven't worn some of your clothes in a while, try them on. There's no point in hauling clothes to college if they don't fit or if you don't like them anymore. Remember the "panty postulate": the more underwear you bring to college, the less often you'll need to do your laundry. Just something to keep in mind. Also, consider the climate. You are going to need different clothing at the University of Vermont than you would need at the University of Texas.

Your Packing Checklist

Draw a line through the following items as you pack them:

Underwear	Waterproof gloves (multiple)
Socks (athletic/dressy)	Wool socks (multiple)
Bras (regular and sport)	Thermal underwear
Pajamas	Waterproof shoes
Comfortable walking shoes	Medications in their original labeled pill bottles, marked with your name, dosage amount, and instructions
Running shoes	
Flip-flops	
Jeans	Toothbrush
T-shirts	Toothpaste
Sweatshirts	Hairbrush
Light jacket	Shampoo
Sweaters	Conditioner
Swimming suit	Hair dryer
Shorts	Deodorant
Dress or shirt and tie	Tweezers
Dressy pants and shirt or blouse	Adhesive bandages
Dressy shoes	Antibiotic cream
Scarf	Nail clippers
Knit hat	Cosmetics
Parka	Sunblock

Make sure you have all your medications refilled before you go to college. You don't want to search for a pharmacy or doctor during your first few weeks of school.

TRANSPORTATION (PLANES, TRAINS, BICYCLES, AND AUTOMOBILES)

If you are living on campus your first year of college, consider leaving your car at home. Most campuses require parking permits, and those permits can be expensive. Besides, parking spaces can be hard to come by on campus, even with a permit. The reason for this is that most campuses sell more parking permits than there are parking spaces. You may have to circle like a vulture around the parking lot in order to find a space.

In desperation, you may be tempted to park illegally on campus, especially when there are no legit spaces available and you are running late for class. Beware the parking ticket! If you ignore it, the next time you park on campus you may get a "boot" on your car—a metal device that the parking enforcement agency locks onto the wheel of your car. The boot will not be taken off your car until your parking tickets have been paid. "Not fair!" you cry. Look at it this way: you are on the college's turf—they can (and will) enforce their rules.

If you need more reasons to leave your car at home, consider the cost, both in money and time, of maintaining a car: oil changes, fuel, and car insurance really add up, and they require time and planning as well. You can always grab a ride to the store (or anywhere else) with a friend or roommate in lieu of using your car.

If you live in an apartment, consider riding the bus to campus rather than driving there. Getting a bus pass is relatively inexpensive. The challenging part may be budgeting extra time to get to campus—you need to get up early enough to get to the bus stop on time, and if you miss the bus, there may not be another scheduled in time for you to get to your class. Another alternative is to ride your bike to campus. Even if you live quite a distance away, you can take advantage of the bicycle racks on the front of many buses. You wait with your bike at the bus stop, the bus arrives, you load on your bike, you get on board, and you're done. Of course, you'll need to take care to learn the rules of bicycle safety before you venture out on campus, and always wear a helmet. Websites that provide guidelines for biking on campus can be found in the Resources section at the end of this book.

In this chapter, you learned about the living arrangements, essential supplies, and transportation options of the typical college student. In the next chapter, you'll learn about college lingo, scheduling tips, setting deadlines, preparing a well-stocked backpack, and finding a major you will actually enjoy.

3

Be at the Top of Your Class

Now that you've settled into your new accommodations, you'll need to register for classes. In this chapter you will learn how to schedule your classes effectively, get the most out of your courses, choose a major, and get to know your professors. You're also about to find out that college comes with its own special set of terms. Words like "course load" and "drop/add" may not sound familiar now, but they will become part of your life soon. After reading this section, you'll be up on the lingo and be able to decipher some common phrases related to college classes, while you're navigating the world of course registration.

YOUR COURSE LOAD

Your "course load" is the amount of classes (or credits) you are taking in a semester. A class that meets for three hours each week is typically worth three credits. You usually need to take between twelve and fifteen credits a semester to qualify as a full-time student. It is important to maintain full-time status in order to retain scholarships and/or continue to be covered by your parents' (or the college's) medical insurance.

However, if you're planning on working while you go to school (this is generally not recommended your first year, but sometimes it is not an option), or if you commute to campus from another city, consider cutting back on your class credits. On the other hand, if you are a person with ADD who does well with a lot of stuff on your plate, this may work for you. But make sure you're leaving yourself enough time to study, relax, and have a social life.

> *Never overextend yourself. Don't be scared to slow down and reduce your course load. If it takes an extra year or two to get through college with a 3.5 GPA versus a 2.8, it will be worth it in the end when you want a job or apply to grad school.*
>
> —Megan, sophomore, University of Florida

DROP/ADD AND WITHDRAWAL

After you register, you can still change your classes during the "drop/add" period, usually two weeks after the semester begins. Being permitted to drop or add classes can be a lifesaver, because sometimes you'll find yourself enrolled in a class that is just not right for you—perhaps the work will simply take more time than you have, you're having some difficulty with the professor, or you're just not succeeding in the class.

Check with your college to get the exact deadline for dropping and adding courses, and make sure you mark it on your calendar. Also, be certain to follow the correct procedure for dropping. If you fail to get the correct signatures or turn in your form on time, you will still be enrolled in the class and you will receive a grade for your work (or lack of work) in it. Keep in mind that you will not get a refund for your class, even if you dropped it during the allotted time period.

If you've done everything possible (including asking the professor if you can do additional work to boost your grade) and you still are failing, you may be able to withdraw the class, or remove it from your schedule.

A "course withdrawal" means you drop a class after the drop/add period is over, resulting in a W on your transcripts. A "medical withdrawal" means that you're withdrawing for the semester due to a medical issue, mental or physical. As is the case with dropping and adding classes, there is a procedure for filing a medical withdrawal. At most colleges, you'll be required to at least provide documentation from a physician stating the reasons that a medical issue prevents you from continuing the semester.

GRADE POINT AVERAGE (GPA)

Your GPA is determined by adding up all of your grades for a particular semester, and then dividing the sum by the number of credits or classes. In some schools, your GPA plays an important part in your ability to continue at that university: once you've completed two years of general education classes, you may have to apply to a particular specialized college, for example, the College of Journalism and Communications, and you need a minimum GPA in order to get into that college. If you don't get in, you'll likely have the opportunity to appeal the decision, or you can apply to a different college within your university. However, it's best to have the required GPA before you apply to the specialized college of your choice, so you can avoid the appeal or reapplication process. Your GPA will also be taken into account when you apply to graduate school, if you choose to do so.

SCHEDULING YOUR CLASSES

Let's talk about the fine art of scheduling. Optimal scheduling can make a huge difference in your academic success, so you'll want to schedule carefully.

First, refrain from scheduling classes on Friday afternoons or Monday mornings. You will most likely not go to these classes as often. Also, schedule your classes based on your body clock. Some people are night owls—they focus better in the afternoon and at night. Some people are more alert in the morning and need downtime in the afternoon. If you are a night owl, schedule your classes from the early afternoon on. If you are an early bird, choose classes that meet in the morning hours.

People with ADD can have difficulty making transitions, so it is recommended that you have one hour between classes. This gives you time to review your notes and rewrite them, stop for a snack, walk to your next class, and, most important, give your brain a break. Breaks lasting more than one hour, however, can lead to increased distraction and difficulty transitioning to your next class. You want to give your brain a rest, not a two-week vacation.

Writing Down Your Class Schedule

In addition to using a planner (see chapter 2), you'll also find it helpful to make a separate weekly schedule that tells you the times of your classes, social activities, and study periods. First, make a copy of the schedule on the next page for each day of the week.

For every time slot, write down your planned activities: class, study time, meetings, and social gatherings. Also make sure you schedule time for errands and free time. Use a different color ink for each activity—red for classes, blue for study time, and so on. Alternatively, you can also create a calendar on a spreadsheet or scheduling program. You don't need to follow the schedule exactly, but it should give you a good idea of how much time you are spending on each activity. It also shows you areas where you may need to reprioritize your time.

Day of the Week: _____

7:00 a.m.	
7:30 a.m.	
8:00 a.m.	
8:30 a.m.	
9:00 a.m.	
9:30 a.m.	
10:00 a.m.	
10:30 a.m.	
11:00 a.m.	
11:30 a.m.	
12:00 p.m.	
12:30 p.m.	
1:00 p.m.	
1:30 p.m.	
2:00 p.m.	
2:30 p.m.	
3:00 p.m.	
3:30 p.m.	
4:00 p.m.	
4:30 p.m.	
5:00 p.m.	
5:30 p.m.	
6:00 p.m.	
6:30 p.m.	
7:00 p.m.	
7:30 p.m.	

GET THE MOST OUT OF YOUR CLASSES

To help yourself study in the most efficient and effective way possible, try the suggestions below. Even if you use only one of these suggestions, your academic performance will likely improve.

Be Prepared

In order to get the most out of class, you need to carry the right tools. You'll want to keep the following items in your backpack at all times:

- A tag with your identifying information. Do not put your apartment number on this tag. Your name, e-mail address, and phone numbers are fine. Put a phone number other than that of your cell on the tag, in case your cell phone is in the bag when it's misplaced.

- Planner

- Notepad

- Pens

- Pencils

- Recording device (minirecorder)

People with ADD have a tendency to cram stuff in their backpacks five minutes before they leave for class. Instead, make a habit of checking your backpack the night before class to make sure you have everything.

I use two backpacks. I have one where I keep my books and folders for my Monday-Wednesday-Friday classes, and one where I keep my stuff for my Tuesday-Thursday classes. That way I can just pick up whichever backpack I need and just go.
　　　　　　　　　　　　　—Bailey, junior, Winthrop University

Heed the Syllabus

A syllabus contains the schedule, assignments, requirements, and policies for a class. The syllabus is handed out on the first day of class, or it is posted online. You are responsible for knowing all the information on the syllabus, including any changes the professor makes to it. When you first get the syllabus for a class, write down all the assignment due dates and test dates in your planner. You can then break down assignments and projects into smaller chunks and schedule these on your planner in order to get things done ahead of time.

Keep a list of all assignments and exams—when they are, etc. This will help you prioritize your work and help you keep an accurate picture of the week or month ahead.
                                    —Taryn, graduate student, University of Florida

Set Your Own Deadlines

It is beneficial to create your own deadlines throughout the semester, especially since people with ADD tend to wait until the last minute to complete big projects. If you have a project due at the end of the semester, you can create monthly goals for yourself to complete smaller parts of the project. Smaller goals for a writing project might include the following:

- Researching the topic

- Making an outline of the information you will include

- Completing a draft

- Creating your final version, printing it, and assembling the paper

If you have both a project due and a final to take during the last week of class, you may want to schedule earlier deadlines for yourself. That way you can finish the project a couple of weeks early, giving yourself time to study for the final.

Record Your Classes

A very helpful way for you to review your classes and improve your notes is to record your lectures. This can be done with a minirecorder. Always check with your professors to see if it is okay to record their lectures. (This is also a good way to introduce yourself to your professor.)

I lost a lot of what was being said in class because of all of the distractions. I found that using a mini cassette recorder and carrying lots of tapes and batteries helped me. I reviewed tapes at the end of the day and I compared notes.
　　　　　　　　—Kathy, sophomore, Santa Fe Community College

Always Attend the "Real" Class

In some of your larger classes, you may have the opportunity to watch the class on TV or via the Internet. In most cases, it's better to attend the actual class, and use the recorded class as a tool for reviewing the lecture. By attending the class, you have quite a few advantages that you wouldn't have if you only viewed the class virtually. It's easier to pay attention, you have an opportunity to ask questions, and you have a better ability to read the nonverbal behaviors of your professor. You're also more likely to take notes if you are surrounded by other students doing the same.

Show up every day, as prepared as possible. Try your best at all times. Never give up, and don't be afraid to ask for extra help. We all need a little extra help sometimes. Listen as carefully as possible to everything your teacher says. If you find it helpful, bring a recorder with you to class, if the professor will allow it. My little brother brought a laptop with him to school so he could type notes faster than he normally can write them. Number one—show up to class no matter what!
　　　　　　　　　　　　—John, senior, University of Florida

Extra Credit

For students who want to succeed in college, there is no such thing as extra credit. Treat all extra credit opportunities as required assignments. Those extra points can make the difference between a B and an A. You can also ask the professor for additional opportunities to earn extra credit.

Internet Classroom Software

Many colleges have software applications that allow your professor to send mass e-mail to the class, post grades, and post slides prior to class for online viewing. You can then print out the slides, look them over, and take them to class, which makes it much easier to follow along with the lecture. Your professor will let you know if he or she will be utilizing this software.

Take Great Notes (or Find Someone to Do It for You)

Having notes from your classes is absolutely essential for your academic success. However, although most people with ADD find that taking notes helps them focus on the class material, others discover that taking notes actually slows their learning process. In that case, you might find a friend who will share notes with you. If you've received accommodations through your college, you can also ask for assistance with note taking. For more information on accommodations, see chapter 5.

If you decide to take notes yourself, listen for cues from your professors that indicate that they're about to make an important point. When your professor says the following phrases, you'll generally want to write down what immediately follows: "The important thing to remember is..."; "The main points are..."; and "In summary...."

Recopy your notes as soon as you finish class. This will help you retain the information. It is best to decipher your handwriting right after class, since it's harder to make sense of your notes a few weeks later.

Compare notes with a classmate to make sure both of you caught the most important parts of the lecture.

An even better way to take notes is to bring your laptop to class. People with ADD commonly have difficulty with handwriting, so it may be easier for you to review typewritten notes than to decipher your handwriting. To make this easier, many classrooms have electrical outlets and wireless Internet access. If you don't know how to type, you can learn using typing software or free typing programs available online, which are listed in the Resources section at the end of this book. As always, remember to keep an eye on your laptop at all times.

Taking Notes When Your Professor Talks Too Fast

You may find that it's difficult for you to take notes when your professor either speaks rapidly or is difficult to understand. By the time you've finished writing down an important concept, the professor is already ten steps ahead of you! Here are some suggestions for making note taking easier when your professor is going a mile a minute.

The most obvious solution is to talk to your professor after class and ask him or her to speak more slowly, or you can review your notes with your professor to catch up on what you missed. If you'll be reviewing notes with your professor (or with a classmate), just focus on writing down the key points during class and leave large spaces on the page below each note. Then you'll fill in the spaces with your more complete notes. Additionally, you might ask to make copies of your classmates' notes afterwards, or record your professors' lectures to aid you in deciphering fast speech (see Record Your Classes, above).

The Brain-Hand Connection

Some people with ADD find that they can come up with an idea for a paper in their head, but translating it into writing can be difficult. If this is an issue for you, try using voice recognition software. These programs allow you to speak into a microphone, and the program types it out for you. You can also dictate your paper to a friend, who can then type it out. Recommended voice recognition programs can be found in the Resources section at the end of this book.

Interacting with Professors

Professors are usually instructors who have earned their Ph.D. Your classes may be taught by a professor or by a graduate student. All of the following suggestions apply regardless of who is teaching the class.

INTRODUCE YOURSELF TO YOUR PROFESSOR AND GO TO OFFICE HOURS

It is important to make yourself known to your professor. Introduce yourself at the first class, and also visit during the professor's office hours (scheduled periods of time when professors are available to provide support to their students). Even if you don't have a test coming up, stop by during office hours anyway—you can always review your assigned reading or upcoming projects with the professor.

I find that turning up to a lecture early and being in the front row helps me. I also ask the teacher if I can have a copy of the lecture notes. I can really fill in the gaps that I missed due to daydreaming.
—Kelly, senior, University of Worcester (England)

WHY YOU SHOULD MEET YOUR PROFESSOR

Meeting with your professor makes it easier for an ADD student to become more interested in the class. It's a positive cycle—the more effort you invest, the more interest you'll have in the class. The more interest you have in a class, the higher your grade will be. In addition, connecting with your professor shows you have an interest in doing well and it gives you an opportunity to ask for a recommendation letter when you need one. You can also have your professor review your assignments before you turn them in, ask for suggestions on how to improve your grade, and receive opportunities to do an assignment for more points—particularly helpful when you're a couple of points away from a higher grade.

Remember that professors are regular people just like you, and they are always happy to see students interested in their classes.

RESEARCH YOUR PROFESSORS AND CLASSES ON THE INTERNET

Thanks to the Internet, you can now view how professors' former students have rated their teaching style; keep in mind that reviews of a professor are not definitive proof of their ability. Ask other students which professors they recommend. If you're interested in a particular field, look on the college's website to view the research interests of the professors. For example, if you'd like to do research on the behavior of squids, you may want to take a class from a professor who has done squid research. A list of websites that rate professors can be found in the Resources section at the end of this book.

Three main things for college success are starting off the semester right, using a website such as ratemyprofessor.com to find out about your profs, and always trying to make it to class. Do these three things and you're well on your way to a successful college experience.

—Brent, junior, University of Florida

CHOOSING A MAJOR

Your major, or track, is your concentrated field of study. It is the field in which you'll receive your degree. Some four-year colleges require that you "declare" your major, or track, in your first year, while others let you wait until your sophomore or even junior year. Choosing your major or track means that you must start meeting course-completion requirements for your degree. Each major has specific courses or categories of courses it requires for you to receive your degree.

It is normal to want to change your major, and people with ADD change majors more often. One of the best ways to narrow down your choices and find the right classes is to visit an academic adviser—a staff member who helps you understand the requirements for your degree, reviews your classes for the next semester to make sure you're on track, and explains any paperwork that's required in order for you to graduate. There are often academic advisers who work in the college or department of your chosen major. Since students with ADD can have difficulty keeping track of their required courses and paperwork, visit your academic adviser as early in your college career as possible, and visit him or her regularly throughout your schooling.

What really worked for me was researching what types of degrees were out there that fit my personality and obviously that could hold my attention. I took a few personality and career aptitude tests that gave me a better base to start at and from those results I ended up at the University of Maine with a BA in adventure recreation business management.

—Adam, senior, University of Maine

How Do You Choose a Major?

You may wonder why you're required to take general education classes that have nothing to do with the major in which you are interested. The reasoning is that, as you are exposed to different fields of study, you will make a more informed choice about your major (and your eventual career path).

Your major is not set in stone. You can change it at any time. However, be aware that if you change your major, you may have to take extra classes in order to graduate. In addition, if you're planning on going to law school or medical school, you'll be required to have particular undergraduate classes.

Earning a degree in a particular field doesn't mean you are locked into getting a job in that field. You can always find a career path that is different from your degree. But pursuing a career that is closely tied to your degree does tend to make things easier for you when you're looking for a job.

Finding a Major

When trying to determine your chosen field of study, you need to educate yourself regarding the available options. Check out the college's undergraduate catalog, either online or in printed form, which lists the majors and required classes. Look through it and see what majors are available. Now, answer the following questions.

1. Quick: write down five majors that interest you the most: _____

    _____

    _____

2. What is it that interests you about each major? _____

    _____

    _____

3. What do these majors have in common? _____

    _____

    _____

4. Do they relate to any interests you have outside of school? _____

    _____

    _____

5. Look at the classes required for each major. Do any of these particularly interest you? _____

    _____

    _____

6. Now look at the college's website, or search online. What kinds of careers are available for each major? _____

    _____

_____

_____

7. Do any of these careers interest you? Which ones? _____

_____

_____

8. Look at the five majors you wrote down in question 1. Have you changed your mind about any of them? _____

_____

9. Rank the majors according to your interest in them, with 1 meaning "most interested" and 5 meaning "least interested." _____

_____

_____

_____

10. For your top choice, seek more information from students with that major, or visit that department for more information. Then go on down the list. Make notes here: _____

_____

_____

_____

11. Review your fact-finding mission with your parents or your academic adviser. How are you feeling about your choices? _____

_____

_____

Haley's Tips for College Success

Haley has some useful tips for you. Listen to her—she knows what she's talking about.

- Don't skip class even if attendance is not taken or if class is optional.

- Study the material as you get it, not at the last minute.

- Try to date all notes and keep them organized, and save them— finals are usually cumulative.

- Sleep eight hours every night and take your meds as prescribed.

- Remember that if you work hard and schedule your time wisely, you will have time to do what you want.

- Take classes you love.

- Eat well, not junk, or you will gain the "freshman twenty."

—Haley, junior, University of Florida

In the next chapter you will learn about two activities that are central to your college experience—studying and taking tests.

4

Testing Your Patience

In this chapter, you will learn about two main features of college life—studying and taking tests. This is the most important part of college, as your grades depend on your productivity, efficiency, and ability to recall information.

STUDYING

Studying is a necessary part of college. Of course, that doesn't mean you have to be happy about it. I'd be worried if you walked into the library and announced, "I'm here, and I'm ready to study! Woo hoo!" Though studying may not necessarily be fun, there are ways to make it less painful.

What Does "Studying" Mean, Anyway?

You know you need to study when you're in college, but what exactly does that mean? When you have ADD, the last thing you want to do is sit and read a textbook. So you may wind up not studying at all. However, there are other ways to study. All "studying" means is that you are familiarizing yourself with the material—and you can do so much more than read a textbook. "Studying" includes:

- Answering the questions at the end of a textbook chapter

- Rewriting and organizing your notes

- Comparing your notes with a classmate's notes

- Reviewing the notes that you've organized

- Doing exercises and examples (even if they haven't been assigned)

- Reading complementary material (Internet or library research)

- Putting the content of your notes and research onto flash cards that you can easily review

- Attending test review sessions given by the professor or instructor

- Receiving tutoring

All of these methods will help you acquire and retain information. Remember that anything you do to help yourself gain knowledge counts as studying.

Tutoring

People with ADD learn most effectively when they get individualized attention. Tutoring is an excellent way to achieve your academic goals. Some benefits of tutoring include getting help with organizing material and keeping you on track with a major project, in addition to helping you identify and focus on the most important areas of your course work. You can hire a private tutor, or you may be able to get tutoring from your college's academic advising center.

PRIVATE TUTORING

You may be able to receive one-on-one instruction from a private tutor, although it will most likely cost you more than getting tutoring on campus will. On the other hand, you usually get what you pay for, so choose tutors carefully, and weigh the importance of saving money over receiving high-quality help.

You may need different tutors for different subjects. Tutors usually get paid an hourly rate and are paid immediately after a tutoring session. To find an effective private tutor, seek recommendations from professors, friends, and your college's academic advising center.

ON-CAMPUS TUTORING

Many campuses have tutoring centers, some even for specific subject areas, such as science or math. Make sure you check the tutor's references. Many campuses also have "writing centers," where students will proofread your papers and give you suggestions for improvement. This may be a free service at your college.

What to Ask the Tutor

When you contact the tutor, ask about the following information:

- Experience in working with ADD students

- Subjects of expertise

- Hourly rate

- Tutoring techniques

- Location of tutoring (Will he or she come to your house?)

- List of references with contact info

Call the tutor's references and ask how long they worked with the tutor, how they got along with the tutor, if the tutor was adaptable to their learning style, and if the tutoring was effective.

HOW TUTORS HELP YOU

Tutors can help you study more effectively for a test by organizing and reviewing your materials with you. They can teach you techniques for more effective absorption of the material, and they can also teach you how to take better notes and give you guidance on writing papers. In addition, they can help you set deadlines and teach you how to break a long assignment into manageable parts. The success of your tutoring is largely dependent on your motivation to work with the tutor—you get out of it what you put into it. If you feel that you don't click with a tutor, go ahead and find another. Your education is too valuable to waste time dealing with frustration over a tutor.

Procrastination

Procrastination is the bane of existence for many people with ADD. In situations where you are putting off work, do the most challenging task first. You are more likely to complete a less desirable task if you know a more desirable task will follow. You may also suffer from perfectionism—you're going to do it perfectly, or you're not going to do it at all. This can be particularly common in people with ADD because they're used to making careless errors. Therefore, they hyperfocus on details, causing their brain to get exhausted, and they lose sight of the big picture. Tell yourself, "Just get it done." Turning it in on time with some errors is almost always better than turning it in late.

Do not put off completing any kind of homework, especially essays. The pressure of completing everything on time will build up, and by the time you get around to starting your homework, you'll be stuck.
—Rebecca, freshman, St. Johns River Community College

Finding a Place to Study

There is no magic place for studying that works for everyone. Anywhere that allows you to be productive and calm is the place where you should study. Locations include the library, an empty classroom, a coffeehouse, outside under a tree, on the bus while you're riding to campus, and at your desk at home.

You may find that you need a few people around so you can stay focused on studying. Sometimes just having one person around can motivate you. Studying with non-ADD people can make you frustrated, but it can also be a good way to learn effective studying techniques. Study with people who are supportive of your need to use alternative studying methods, since sitting still at a table for hours at a time may not necessarily work for you.

To really be able to learn and focus on material, I had to isolate myself on the top floor of the library. The floor with the really, really old journals that nobody would ever want to read. I would go with only the material I wanted to learn, and then I had absolutely nothing that could distract me. I would not let myself leave until I got it done.

—Matt, senior, University of Wyoming

STUDYING AT HOME

If you study at home, make it very clear to your roommates that you need quiet. This can be done first by telling them you are going to study, and then by putting a "do not disturb" sign on your door. Having someone keep an eye on you can help you focus on studying, so you might ask one of your roommates to be your "studying coach." That way, if you wander out of your room, your roommate can kick you right back in there (not literally). Return the favor by doing something helpful for your roommate. You will learn more about bartering in chapter 8.

If you get distracted by noises at home, try a "white noise" machine or CD, or a ceiling fan—these may produce enough noise to keep you focused. Resources for white noise machines and CDs can be found in the Resources section at the end of this book.

You may have been told that listening to music while studying is a big no-no. However, music can actually improve your ability to focus. (Your parents can hear you cry "I told you so" from here.) If you study better with music, then your room is a great place for working, especially if you like listening to loud music. Remember that people can sometimes hear your music through your headphones if you are studying at a library or other quiet place. At home, make sure you wear headphones (consider noise-canceling headphones) so as to not disturb your roommates.

One of the advantages of studying at home is that you have all the creature comforts. But always sit at your desk instead of on your bed or couch—you are more likely to stay awake if you study at your desk. And staying awake is one of those key features of effective studying.

I usually study in my room, unless I'm studying for finals or working on a research paper. When that's the case, I'll work in the library.

—Lauren, sophomore, Bucknell University

Scheduling Your Study Time

Your "body clock" was mentioned in chapter 3 in a discussion regarding how to schedule classes effectively. This is also important when you are determining your studying schedule. Are you most alert in the morning or afternoon? Schedule your study time for when you are most awake and focused. If you study while you're having a lull in energy, you may read your textbook but not absorb what you're reading. If you are awake and focused, you will have a more productive study session.

Study Each Day

For each hour of class time per week, you need to schedule at least one hour of study time per day. Schedule your study time on your planner. If you study every day, you'll find it easier to pick up where you left off the day before instead of spending an hour trying to figure out what you've already studied.

Cramming at the last minute is a gamble. There's a possibility that you will oversleep and miss your test because you stayed up too late studying. Even if you are awake for your test, this doesn't mean that all the cylinders are running. You may be there physically, but not mentally. If you feel you are getting tired while studying, by all means go to sleep. You will continue to process and "consolidate" information in your memory while you sleep (Ellenbogen et al. 2006). So think of sleep as studying without any extra effort.

I noticed that with the stress of preparing for exams, especially around finals, it became hard to get decent sleep and hard to focus. To try to minimize distractions, I went to the medical school library on campus and parked myself in the stacks at one of the oversized desks. Once there, the fatigue would catch up with me and I would fall asleep. I noticed that when I woke up a short time later, I was relaxed and focused. I could study and retain information very well for tests.

—Susan, senior, Indiana University

How to Study

Before you start studying, follow these steps in order to be more effective. First, clear off your desk. If you have a lot of stuff on your desk, put it in a temporary holding place, like a crate or bin—less clutter means more focused attention. You can always put your stuff back on your desk after you study. Next, gather your study supplies together: get a legal pad, your textbook, a pen, and a highlighter. Pour yourself a large glass of water; your brain works better when it's hydrated. Then use the bathroom, so you're not distracted by a full bladder.

Next, set up a study rhythm. Studying for small increments of time works for most people with ADD. Get a kitchen timer and set it for thirty minutes. Study for the entire thirty minutes. When the timer goes off, stop studying, no matter what—people with ADD have a tendency to hyperfocus and can get exhausted if they don't take regular breaks. Now, set the timer for fifteen minutes. This is your study break.

During your study break, engage in one of the following activities in order to refresh yourself: take a walk, get a snack, take a shower, or call an upbeat friend.

When the timer goes off, get right back to studying and start the process over again. If you need an extra boost, before you start studying ask your roommate to kick you back into play if you wander away from your desk.

Go to the library every day to study, even if it is just for an hour. You'll be surprised at how much you'll get done by doing this.
　　　　　—Taryn, graduate student, University of Florida

Your Learning Style

Everyone has his or her own style of learning. In the next section, you will learn tips and techniques geared for the way your brain learns. First, however, we need to find out your learning style.

Learning Style Quiz

For each question, select the answer that best applies to you.

1. When I'm studying, I prefer
   a. Studying alone with just my notes and a book
   b. Talking over points with a study group
   c. Working with one other person so we can take the information and act it out

2. The following item is most useful to have with me when studying:
   a. A highlighter
   b. An MP3 player with my favorite music
   c. An object that represents what I'm studying

3. I learn best when my professor
   a. Writes key points on the board
   b. Discusses key points
   c. Demonstrates key points

4. I remember things best when
   a. I write them down
   b. I record them and play them back
   c. I act them out

5. I retain information best when
   a. I can look at maps and diagrams
   b. I can put the information in a rhyme or song
   c. I can watch a demonstration

6. If a friend recommended a restaurant in an unfamiliar town, I would
   a. Ask him to draw me a map
   b. Ask him to tell me how to get there
   c. Just set out in the general direction of the restaurant

7. When I assemble furniture from a box, I usually

   a. Read the directions and follow the diagrams

   b. Have a friend read the directions to me

   c. Just put it together without using the directions

8. During a trip for spring break, if my cousin asked me what college was like, I would most likely

   a. Show her photos

   b. Tell her about it

   c. Take her there if it were close enough

If you chose *a* most often, then you have a predominately visual learning style. If you answered with mostly *b*'s, then you have a predominately auditory learning style. If you selected mostly *c*'s, then you have a predominately kinesthetic learning style. Keep reading to find out how to study to your advantage according to the way you learn.

Finding the optimal way to study depends on how you best absorb information. Some people learn best when they can see the information in front of them, other people learn best when they're listening to the information, while still others learn best when they can have more of an interactive experience with the material. Let's look at some clues to help you figure out which best describes how you learn most effectively.

VISUAL LEARNING

People who are visual learn most effectively using their eyes. They excel at learning from the following:

- Written directions

- Videos

- Charts and diagrams

- Reading

- Remembering faces

- Showing or drawing things for others

Visual learners will increase their studying effectiveness by copying their notes, using flash cards, and color coding—which can also help you get your materials together for class.

The cabinet of many colors. Purchase a file cabinet with drawers of different colors, ideally on wheels, because rolling carts can be relocated easily. Assign each drawer to represent a different class. Carry that color theme through to your folders and notebooks. For example, if you are putting your English class materials in the red drawer, use a red notebook and red binder just for that class. This makes it much easier to stay organized. People with ADD can be very visually oriented, and keeping everything color coded cuts down on the time you spend searching for your class materials.

> *Develop a system that personally works for you. I have found that creating and using a color-coded highlighting system works best for me to jog my memory about important facts. Also essential is making and studying my own flash cards—forget about using ready-made flash cards! Writing down the information and studying it in my own handwriting seems to cement it in my brain. Also get involved in very proactive small study groups—this helps fill in gaps in your notes.*
> —Sue, junior, University of Florida

AUDITORY LEARNING

Auditory people learn most when they use their ears. They excel at learning from:

- Verbal directions

- Videos

- Lectures

- Music

- Remembering names

- Explaining things to others

If you are an auditory learner, you'll increase your ability to retain information by discussing class material with others, recording lectures, and reading your lecture notes aloud.

As you might imagine, video instruction works best for both auditory and visual learners, since it combines both visual and auditory cues. If you're not sure which learning style you have, try different techniques until you find a good match.

KINESTHETIC LEARNING

Kinesthetic learners retain material best through hands-on activities. They learn best when someone shows them how to do something. If they can also participate in the activity, they learn the material even quicker. Kinesthetic learners excel at the following:

- Demonstrations

- Labs

- Role plays

- Performing

- Learning information while moving around

Kinesthetic learners can benefit from acting out skits about the material they are learning, building a model, or even simply walking around while learning material.

Studying Techniques

You want to acquire and retain the greatest amount of information in the most efficient use of time. Consider the following tips for making the most out of your studying time.

STUDY GROUPS

For some people with ADD, study groups are the most effective way to study. Discussing the material with other people, explaining it to someone, and listening to others' ideas are all beneficial ways to absorb information. Small study groups can also be helpful because you are accountable to others—if you know people are watching, you're more likely to study.

Be aware of the kind of relationship you have with the members of the group before you start studying. Will you study, or will you wind up socializing instead? Can the group help rein you in if you get distracted? You need not disclose to the group that you have ADD, as long as you know your distraction triggers.

When utilizing a study group, limit the total number of people in the group to no more than four or five. Having more than a few people in a group can lead to distractions and will increase the likelihood that the study group will turn into a major social activity. However, a little socializing can actually make studying more enjoyable and productive. Study groups can be particularly helpful when you're completing projects for a class. You can be a major asset to the group, too, since people with ADD are great at coming up with ideas—they just need other people in the group to help bring their ideas to fruition.

How to Work with a Study Group

Try some of the following techniques for making the most of your study group.

- Set ground rules. Who is the group leader? What's the policy for people who arrive late to the group?

- Meet at the same time and day of the week for each session, so it's easier for everyone to remember.

- Have each group member come up with five questions that might be on the test.

- Have each person present a specific topic to the group when you are studying for a test.

- Compare notes so you can fill in gaps.

- Quiz each other using questions in the back of the book.

- Review the effectiveness of the group. How has each of you done on the tests?

CONTEXT-DEPENDENT LEARNING

Studies have shown that if you study in the same location where you will take your test, you will recall the information better during the test itself; this is called "context-dependent learning." Since you won't always be able to study right in the classroom, you could try the same idea with scent. For example, wear a certain perfume or cologne only when you're studying. If you wear that scent when you take the test, you may be able to recall more information (Smith and Vela 2001). You may also want to use a "lucky charm" when studying and then have that lucky charm with you when you take the test (just make sure your lucky charm isn't contraband). If your ADD medication was in your system while you were studying, make sure it's in your system when you take the test. Basically, you want to replicate the environment in which you studied as completely as possible.

While you are studying, eat or drink something with a distinctive flavor, but it has to be something that can be consumed during

the test. I used to chomp on the same flavor of candy during class,
studying, and tests for given subjects, like organic chemistry.
—Susan, senior, Indiana University

IMPROVING READING COMPREHENSION

A common feature of ADD is lack of comprehension: reading the same page over and over and just not absorbing what you're reading. There are a few solutions to this frequent ADD challenge. First, if you find yourself reading something and not absorbing it, take a break. The neurotransmitters in your brain need a rest. Do a task that has nothing to do with reading, like running or listening to music.

Second, once your brain has returned from its minivacation, attempt to read again; this time, as you read, use a piece of paper to cover up the words you haven't gotten to yet. Lower the piece of paper as you read.

Third, if you are assigned a novel to read, consider reading a study guide version before you read the actual book. Yes, you still have to read the actual book! But reading a synopsis of the book beforehand will help you absorb more information from the book.

Fourth, after you've finished reading a book, discuss it with a friend and write down the key points. This will help you further secure the information in your memory.

Finally, medication for ADD can also help you absorb information in a more efficient manner. You'll learn more about that in chapter 6.

Read Effectively

Make copies of the following form and fill it out as you finish each chapter in your textbook or assigned novel. If you prefer to type out your answers, that's okay too.

Date: _____

Book: _____

Chapter: _____

1. Skim the chapter. No heavy reading—just look through it. Pay attention to the headings, subheadings, and boldface phrases or words. What are some of the topics or ideas that will be covered in this chapter?

     _____

     _____

2. Write down questions you think might be answered in this chapter—for example, "What are the key points?" and "Where did this event take place?"

     _____

     _____

3. Read the chapter one page at a time and look for answers to the questions you wrote under item 2, above. Highlight the main sentence in each paragraph.

4. After you've read half of the chapter, write down or type out what you've learned.

5. Take a short break, and then finish up with the rest of the chapter.

6. After you've finished the chapter, check the questions you wrote for item 2. Did you answer the questions? If not, do so now. Also, reread parts of the chapter that seemed confusing. If most of the chapter seemed confusing, review it with a friend.

THE BEAUTY OF INDEX CARDS

Index cards are inexpensive and portable, and they make great flash cards. Buying index cards that are already attached with a spiral makes it easier to flip through the cards. Make sure you also have your roommate or a friend quiz you. When you quiz yourself, you may (without intending to) sneak a peek at the cards.

You can use flash cards in many ways. For example, if you're studying for a vocabulary test, write the vocabulary word on one side of the card and the definition on the other side of the card. Or, let's say you're studying about slugs, and you need to learn the names of three kinds of slugs: the great grey slug, the banana slug, and the red slug (yes, those are actual slug names). One side of your index card would read:

Name three types of slugs

The other side would read:

Great Grey Slug
Banana Slug
Red Slug

Your roommate would hold up the card and read the question. You would then guess the names of your three slug friends. If you get the question right, you can eliminate that index card during the next round of quizzing.

USE MEMORY GAMES

A *mnemonic device* is a memory aid disguised as a game. An example of a mnemonic device is "Roy G. Biv," which helps you remember the colors of the rainbow, using the first letter of each color: red, orange, yellow, green, blue, indigo, and violet. As you can see, a mnemonic device need not be logical. In fact, the sillier a mnemonic device is, the easier it is to remember. You might also make up a story to go along with list items. For example, let's say you need to remember the names of the first four planets: Mercury, Venus, Earth, and Mars. Make up a story that incorporates the names of the planets—a trip to space, for example. You flew on a Mercury spaceship, and you were seated next to a girl named Venus. You called Earth to let them know you were doing okay, and you ate a Mars bar after you arrived.

> I study differently depending on the class, but usually there's an exam review or practice test given out. For subjects like chemistry and math, practice is really important, so I will do the reviews at the end of the chapters in the book. I have studied in groups with friends for exams where we went over the [exam] review and asked each other questions. I have definitely reviewed my notes from class for every exam. I think my notes and the study guides are the most important for studying.
>
> —Nathalie, freshman, University of South Florida

Staying Focused While Studying

Sitting on a large, inflatable "stability ball" (or Swiss ball) when you are at your desk can help you remain focused. It gives you just enough concentrated distraction to allow you to focus on what you're reading. You may also want to hold on to a Koosh ball while sitting at your desk. If you want to be discreet, you can use a smaller Koosh ball—that way, your friends are less likely to ask you about your little "friend" studying with you. As long as some part of you is moving, your brain will stay focused more easily.

Medication and Studying

If your doctor has prescribed medication to help reduce your ADD symptoms (usually a stimulant), schedule a time to study when you know your medication is in effect. Extended-release stimulants, for example, are usually effective for eight to twelve hours.

Some people take another dose of their stimulant medication at night if they are studying for a test. However, be aware that this may lead to insomnia (and you may run out of medication before the end of the month). Always take your medication only as it has been prescribed to you. In addition, keep in mind that your meds don't work entirely on their own—eating well, getting enough rest, and exercising regularly help boost the effectiveness of your medication. If you feel that your medication is not effective in helping you study, make an appointment with your doctor to have your dosage evaluated.

TESTS

Just like studying, tests are a necessary part of the college experience. They are a way for your professors to see how well you've retained information and how well you are able to apply that information—nothing more, nothing less. They aren't a judgment of your value as a person, nor are they a life sentence of doom. In the past, you may have had difficulty performing on tests because you couldn't focus, or you may have had anxiety that caused your mind to go blank. In this section, you will learn tips and tricks for increasing your performance on tests.

Types of Tests

Tests are usually given all through the semester, with a cumulative test called a final exam given on the last week of class. Although tests come in a variety of formats, multiple choice and essay tests are the most common testing formats in college. In the following pages, you'll find some tips to help you make the grade on these common kinds of tests.

Multiple choice tests usually offer you four or more possible answers for each question. The bummer is that only one of these answers is the correct one. Here's how to ease the pain of multiple choice tests:

■ Your first guess is often the correct guess. If you're torn between two choices, go with your gut reaction.

- Immediately draw a line through the answers you know are incorrect.

- Pay special attention to the word "not" in any test question. If you find a "not," draw a box around it.

- Answers that contain the words "only," "all," or "never" are usually not the right answer.

- If you have no idea what the answer is, choose the middle or longest answer.

When taking an essay test, you need to write an accurate, clear, organized, and grammatically correct answer in a limited time frame. Sometimes you'll be asked to answer just one question using the entire test period, and sometimes you'll need to answer several questions. You may be instructed to bring a test booklet with you to the test; you can purchase these at your campus bookstore. Although your approach to each essay test will differ depending on the number of questions, how long you're given to construct your essays, and how detailed the professor wants your responses to be, here are some suggestions for making essay tests more tolerable:

- Make sure your name is on the cover of your test booklet or on your paper.

- Figure out how much time you can spend on each question. Write that amount of time next to the test question.

- Read the question and underline the key words and questions.

- Spend half of the time allotted per question to write an outline of your answer.

- Spend the rest of the allotted time writing out your answer.

- Start your essay with an introductory sentence.

- Next, state what you will be talking about in your essay.

- Then answer the test question.

- Finally, summarize in one or two sentences.

- Review all of your answers for grammatical and factual errors.

Preparing for Tests

When you have ADD, you are more likely to feel anxious and have difficulty finding important items (like your keys) on the morning of the test. For this reason, a big part of your testing success has nothing to do with studying: taking care of yourself and preparing for test day can be equally as important as hitting the books. In this section, you will learn some nonacademic ways to increase your chances of success.

THE NIGHT BEFORE THE TEST

Get as much sleep as possible before a test. Set your alarm clock, and then turn it around so you cannot see what time it is. If you are nervous and are worrying that you won't sleep, tell yourself that you're just going to close your eyes and rest—watching the time on the clock will only increase your anxiety. You may fear that you won't be able to sleep at all; in that event, just tell yourself that you can always catch up on your sleep after the test. Rest assured: if you've been studying every day (hint, hint) and you know the material well, a lack of sleep will not make that much of an impact.

> If you have to be in a lecture early and don't have the confidence to know you will be on time, ask a friend to phone you to get you up and awake. If need be, get someone to travel with you until you're physically in the lecture.
> —Lea, freshman, Leeds Metropolitan University, England

Preparing Yourself the Night Before the Test

The more items you have prepared the night before, the less you have to think about the next day. Make sure you have the following all ready to go the night before the test:

- ☐ Your entire outfit for the next day is laid out.

- ☐ Your medication is set out in a place where you will see it in the morning and will remember to take it.

Your backpack should contain:

- ☐ Two pens and two pencils

- ☐ Your photo ID and/or school ID

- ☐ Essay booklet if needed

- ☐ Some snacks

- ☐ House keys/car keys

- ☐ Flash cards and/or notes

- ☐ Bottle of water (make sure it's tightly closed and stashed in a pocket on the outside of your backpack)

There are three items I must have before leaving my home: my wallet, phone, and keys. I refer to these items as the "trifecta" or "triple threat." If I ever leave without one or more of these items I feel naked and paranoid that I've lost the item. These items are of importance to me because they are all used daily and would be of great difficulty to replace if lost. Not to mention [the fact that] my father would be furious with me and then lecture me on the virtue of responsibility, which in itself makes it worth double-checking that I have the "trifecta" before leaving.

—Kelley, junior, University of Florida

THE DAY OF THE TEST

Follow your regular routine the day of the test. If you usually exercise in the morning, then exercise on the morning of the test as well. Make sure you eat a healthy breakfast, even if you're in a hurry, and remember to take your ADD medication at the usual time. If you are prone to anxiety, don't arrive at the classroom too early—if a classmate were to ask you a question about a topic on the test and you didn't have the answer, it could kick your anxiety into overdrive.

Perform a calming ritual before you take a test. Deep breathing can be particularly helpful. Stop for some water at a drinking fountain, take a few deep breaths, and repeat to yourself, "I am calm, intelligent, and well prepared for this test." Remember that a test is just a measurement of how well you have understood the information. It is not an evaluation of your worth, nor is it a comment on your abilities.

Review Your Tests with Your Professor

After you get your test back, review it with your professor during his or her office hours. Doing so accomplishes a couple of goals. First, it helps you learn the material even better, and learning from your errors will help you on future exams. Second, it makes your professor more aware of who you are, and it helps him to understand that you really care about doing your best in the class.

Tests are an ongoing part of college life, and, as you know, they can generate a fair amount of anxiety. If you've tried relaxation techniques and you still have difficulties sleeping the night before the test, have anxiety-related symptoms like headaches or stomachaches, or your mind goes blank when you're taking the test, see a mental health professional for counseling and/or medication. There's no need to let anxiety rule your life and affect your academic performance.

In the next chapter, you will learn about the campus services available to students diagnosed with ADD. You'll also learn about your legal rights as a student with a disability.

5

Accommodations Are Your Friend

As a college student with ADD, you may qualify for special accommodations—changes to the class or testing procedures in order to provide students with disabilities equal access to education. Please note that the laws detailed in this chapter apply to both U.S. citizens and foreign students studying in the United States. For information on Canadian student rights, see the Resources section at the end of this book.

WHAT ARE ACCOMMODATIONS?

Accommodations are specific adaptations, mandated by the college at your request, that give you the help that you and other students with learning disabilities need in order to succeed. To put it another way, accommodations create an even playing field—with accommodations, you are on an equal standing with non-ADD students. A study showed that students with ADD saw a significant improvement in their grades when they implemented accommodations. Not only that, but each accommodation was found to be helpful (Trammell 2003), which indicates that even a single accommodation can be beneficial. To be given accommodations, you need to register with the college's Office of Student Disability Services (OSDS). You'll learn more about the registration process later in this chapter.

*Each semester I get a letter and then present it to the teachers,
and the teachers and I come up with a plan on when to take tests
or have papers done. I went from a D to an A in my physics class
because I got accommodations.*
— Jeff, senior, University of Florida

The following accommodations can be helpful for students with ADD:

- Extra time on tests, including standardized tests such as the GRE

- Permission to take tests in a separate and quiet location

- Altered test formats

- Extended time to complete assignments

- Instructions given in writing

- Assistance with reading assignments

- Permission to record lectures and access to recording equipment

- Assistance with writing class notes

- Priority in class registration

- Reduced course load

Note that requests for accommodations for standardized tests such as the Graduate Record Examinations (GRE) need to be filed with that specific testing entity. Contact information for various testing entities is available in the Resources section at the end of this book.

I registered with the student disabilities office, and I found that accommodations helped me cope better with my ADD.
In particular, I got extended time for written assignments.
　　　　　　　　　　—John, graduate student, University of Florida

WHEN SHOULD YOU SEEK ACCOMMODATIONS?

If any of the following apply to you, consider requesting accommodations:

- You received services in high school or at another college and you found them to be very helpful.

- You have tried seeking informal accommodations or exceptions on your own, and you are facing challenges.

- In order to work to your potential, you need extra time on standardized tests.

- You feel your college experience will be more frustrating if you don't have additional help.

THE BURDEN OF PROOF IS ON YOU

For students in elementary school through high school, according to federal law, it is the school's responsibility to identify students who need additional services. However, in college, it is up to you to seek out these services. This may be a new experience for you. Throughout this chapter, you'll learn about your rights and how to be an advocate for yourself—a skill that will serve you well all of your life.

Office of Student Disability Services

The Office of Student Disability Services (OSDS) is a department on campus that provides and coordinates accommodations and services for students who have registered with the office. The OSDS also provides advocacy and support for disabled students. The Office of Student Disability Services may also be known as Student Support Services, the Disability Services Office, or Services to Students with Disabilities. The OSDS is usually part of the Department of Student Services or Department of Academic Services.

Registering with the OSDS is voluntary—you are by no means required to report to your college that you have ADD. However, you may consider notifying the OSDS if you've tried other methods of accommodation without any success.

The OSDS Registration Process

First, to receive services through the OSDS, you will need to provide documentation from a medical professional stating that you do in fact have ADD. The amount of paperwork required depends on the college. Many colleges require proof of testing and accommodations recommended by a mental health professional, and all will require information about how your ADD affects your academic performance.

You may have received services in high school through either an Individualized Education Plan (IEP) or Section 504. Your high school may have also provided you with a "Summary of Performance" if you were enrolled in exceptional education services. The Summary of Performance identifies a student's disability, accommodations provided by the school, the progress to date, and services that need to be continued. You can provide the college with this documentation, but that documentation alone will not be enough to qualify you for accommodations. The college may request that you have a current evaluation done before they grant accommodations. If this is the case, the school does not have to pay for the evaluation. That will be your responsibility.

It is very important that you provide the specific paperwork that your college requires. Requirements may vary among colleges.

WHAT WILL YOU NEED TO PRESENT TO THE OSDS?

Most college campuses require a letter from a mental health professional detailing your diagnosis and how it influences your academic functioning; an evaluation (completed within the past five years) by a mental health professional, with a diagnosis, date of evaluation, relevant testing results, and recommended accommodations; and a copy of your 504 plan or IEP from high school.

Here's a checklist of steps you need to take in order to register with the OSDS. Check the items off as you go.

- ☐ Contact your college's OSDS office.

- ☐ Receive application for services and fill it out.

- ☐ Receive list of possible accommodations.

- ☐ Obtain copy of your ADD evaluation. If you don't have a recent evaluation, contact your doctor or the OSDS for a referral.

- ☐ Obtain copy of your 504 plan, IEP, or Summary of Performance from high school, if applicable.

- ☐ Review and select the accommodations that you feel would be most beneficial to you. For additional help, look at the evaluator's recommendations given in the evaluation report and the accommodations listed in your 504 plan or IEP, if applicable.

- ☐ Submit all paperwork to the OSDS.

- ☐ If you don't hear from the OSDS in a reasonable amount of time, call them for an update.

What the evaluation report needs. There are specific things a college requires in an evaluation. First, the evaluation must be conducted and written by a qualified professional, such as a psychiatrist or psychotherapist. Ask the OSDS or your doctor for a list of recommended evaluators. For the purposes of being registered with the OSDS, the evaluation report should contain:

- A current diagnosis

- The date of the diagnosis

- How the diagnosis was found (evaluation and/or testing)

- The professional's credentials (degrees, board certifications, licenses)

- A statement about how ADD affects one or more of your major life activities (school, work, or home)

- An explanation of how ADD specifically affects your academic performance

- A list of recommended accommodations/services

Include your IEP or Section 504 plan from high school with the rest of your paperwork, since it can be helpful to those determining what accommodations you may need.

You need to be your own advocate during the time when your paperwork is reviewed for approval. Ask the OSDS contact about the people who review your paperwork. What are their credentials and titles? What is the appeals process if your request for accommodations is denied? Also ask about what happens to your paperwork after it's been reviewed. If your request for services is not approved, ask to pick up your paperwork from the office.

WHAT EXACTLY IS A "TIMELY MANNER"?

Legally, a decision regarding your application for accommodations must be provided in a "timely manner"; however, the specific amount

Having a Diagnosis of ADD Is Not Enough

Two court decisions were handed down in 2006, in cases where students had produced evaluations stating they had ADD or a learning disability, following their dismissal from medical school for failing grades. In both cases, the court ruled that a diagnosis was not enough for the student to be covered under the ADA law; the court felt that there was not enough evidence of impairment.

The lesson to be learned from these cases is that you need to register with the OSDS as soon as possible. In both of these cases, the students provided documentation only after they had been dismissed from medical school. Also, you need to not only have a diagnosis but also prove (and the evaluation needs to show) that ADD significantly impairs your functioning.

of time that qualifies as timely is not mentioned in the law. Contact the OSDS after a couple of weeks if you haven't heard from them.

EXCEPTIONS TO ACCOMMODATIONS

Although a college professor may be required to give you extra time on a test, he or she is not required to change the actual composition of the test. The college is also not required to grant accommodations that "would fundamentally alter the nature of a service, program or activity or would result in financial or administrative burdens" (U.S. Department of Education, Office for Civil Rights 2007). The college is also not required to provide personal assistants, readers outside of class time, private tutoring, or typing classes.

You may not be granted all the accommodations you request, but the college usually makes an effort to grant as many accommodations as possible. When you make a list of accommodations you'll be requesting, underline the ones that are nonnegotiable for you. Nonnegotiable accommodations for ADD might include extended time for taking tests, permission to take tests in a quiet location, and priority in class registration. Remember, your college staff and administrators want you to succeed—they are usually invested in your ability to have a good college experience.

ADDITIONAL AVAILABLE SERVICES

Some campuses have writing centers where, for no charge, your papers can be reviewed before you turn them in. They may also offer sessions to help you learn how to write an outline, how to write a term paper, and much more. You may not need to be registered with the OSDS to take advantage of this service. Call the writing center to find out what specific services they provide.

Once You Have Been Registered and Approved

After you have been notified of the approval of your paperwork, you will most likely meet with a staff member of the OSDS to discuss which accommodations you feel will best help you. You may be given a letter from the OSDS stating your name and the accommodations that are required. You'll need to give your professors a copy of this letter so they are aware of the accommodations to which you are entitled. You can meet with your professors after class or during office hours to give them this note.

I got tested and the disability office was helpful because it allowed me to study differently, without judgment. I was quickly accepted as a different type of learner, and I could learn at my own pace while still being able to do the work and take the exams.

—Val, senior, Rollins College

ADVOCATING FOR YOURSELF

Being an advocate for yourself means that you speak up for your rights and needs and are comfortable asking questions and talking to people in authority, even challenging them if necessary, in a productive and respectful way. The best way to be an advocate is to educate yourself about your rights as a college student with ADD. People will ask you questions about why you feel you need services. Some may even tell you that ADD doesn't exist. By being an effective advocate, you take care of yourself and set limits.

Effective self-advocates share several characteristics. They tend to be knowledgeable about ADD, they know how ADD affects their learning and academic performance, and they can articulate why they need accommodations. They also know what accommodations will work best for them. They know their rights and are able to speak assertively but respectfully. In addition, they know the chain of command and understand when they are speaking to someone with limited power. They believe in compromise but also in meeting their needs.

Questions You Will Need to Answer

When you are an advocate for your rights, you need to be able to give answers to the following questions, which you may be asked by college staff or professors. Write out the answers and then practice saying them out loud.

1. What is ADD?

2. How does ADD affect your learning?

3. What specific problems have you had in school?

4. What accommodations did you use in high school?

5. What accommodations do you think can help you in college?

6. How will the accommodations help you?

7. What are your strengths? In what areas do you excel?

8. What techniques have you already tried on your own?

APPLICABLE LAWS

Two federal laws or statutes pertain to college students with ADD (or any disability), and they're discussed below. Keep in mind that you are only covered under these laws if you've filed the proper paperwork with and have been approved by the OSDS at your college.

Title II, Section 202, of the Americans with Disabilities Act (ADA) states that public entities (including public colleges) cannot discriminate against you solely due to your disability. It states, "No qualified individual with a disability shall by reason of such disability be excluded from participation in or be denied the benefits of the services, programs, or activities of a public entity, or be subjected to discrimination by any such entity."

What this means is that your college cannot deny you admission solely based on the fact that you have ADD. They cannot bar you from taking a specific class just because you have ADD, nor can they raise your tuition because you're registered with the OSDS.

According to the ADA, a person who qualifies as having a disability is one who has a physical or mental impairment that substantially limits one or more of his or her life activities, and has a record of his or her impairment. Records of impairment include medical documentation, an IEP, or an evaluation.

Section 504 is part of the Rehabilitation Act of 1973. Section 504 states that a program receiving federal funds cannot discriminate against you because of your disability.

How Do These Laws Apply to Private Colleges?

You'll notice that these laws apply to colleges that either receive public funding or are public entities. So, even if private colleges receive a small amount of funding from the federal government, they are still subject to the ADA and Section 504.

While Title II of the ADA does not apply to a private college without any federal funding, Title III of the ADA does apply. It states that any course must be modified to be accessible to those with a disability. This includes extending time permitted to complete the course, or allowing extra time to turn in assignments (as long as those accommodations are on file for the student at the OSDS). This means that if you're attending a private college, you can still receive accommodations under federal law, even if the college doesn't receive federal funding.

Title III also states that any private college that offers an exam or course related to "licensing, certification, or credentialing for secondary or post secondary education, professional or trade purposes must offer such examinations or courses in a place and manner accessible to persons with disabilities, or offer alternative accessible arrangements for such individuals" (ADA, P.L. 101-336, 42 U.S.C. 12181 et seq.).

The Family Educational Rights and Privacy Act (FERPA) is the federal law that governs parents' access to their child's educational records. Once you turn eighteen or enter college—and your parents no longer claim you as a dependent—those rights transfer to you, the student. This means that your parents do not have a legal right to access your records.

You might be thinking that this is a good thing; actually, allowing your parents access to your records can be very helpful to you. Your parents can give you added support during the OSDS process, and they'll be able to do some of the legwork for you. To allow your parents access to your records, you'll need to sign a "release of information" form with the college. Ask the disabilities office or student services for this form.

ISSUES WITH ACCOMMODATIONS

As with any service you receive in life, you may run across challenges. Here are some of the issues that students may face when seeking accommodations.

Being Denied Accommodations by the OSDS

Even if you've turned in the necessary paperwork, there is no guarantee that the OSDS will approve your request to be registered as a student with a disability. During the review process, the committee may decide that you did not demonstrate an impairing level of ADD, or that you do not have academic impairment. In any case, the OSDS is required to tell you why you were not approved.

Issues with Recording Lectures

Even if the OSDS does approve your application, you may occasionally run into difficulties in actually getting the accommodations you requested. For example, professors may have concerns about you recording their lectures. They may tell you that it's a violation of their rights or other students' rights, or that their lectures are their intellectual property. However, according to Section 504 laws, if taping lectures is an accommodation you have been granted through the OSDS, then you have a right to do so. The college may ask you to sign a form stating that you will only use the recordings for your personal use and will not violate the copyright (for example, by putting the lectures on file-sharing software).

Professors Not Complying with Accommodations

Rarely, you may encounter a professor who doesn't honor your accommodations. First, it is important to determine if the professor is deliberately denying you your required accommodations or if he or she is simply not aware of your required accommodations. There is quite a difference between deliberately denying accommodations and just not being aware of them. First, you need to make sure your professor was notified of your accommodation with a letter from the OSDS. In most cases, if a professor is not aware of the accommodations, all you need to do is discuss the issue with him or her—give the professor the benefit of the doubt. If you weren't given extra time on a test the first time around, you should be allowed to make up this test and have the new score count instead of the previous score.

If, after talking with your professor, you feel the issue has still not been resolved, find out how to file a complaint, and follow the proper procedures for filing a grievance with the OSDS. If you follow the correct grievance procedures and are still not satisfied with the results, have exhausted all other avenues, or believe that your legal rights have been violated, you can file a complaint with the U.S. Department of Education, Office of Civil Rights. The contact information can be found in the Resources section at the end of this book. In any of these scenarios, do consider obtaining legal representation, but keep in mind that pursuing legal action is costly—draining not only your finances but also your emotions and time.

What If the Accommodations Aren't Working?

Sometimes you may not know how well an accommodation will work until you try it out. You may find that some accommodations need to be tweaked or changed altogether. To make changes, see the OSDS as soon as possible. It's much easier and more beneficial for you to have changes made during the semester than to wait until your classes are over.

Keep in mind that you are in charge of having your status or accommodations reviewed or changed. Unlike your high school, where your IEP or Section 504 plan was reviewed each year by the school, your college does not automatically renew or review your status with the OSDS each year. If you need to make changes to your plan, you need to take the initiative in contacting the OSDS.

IF YOU HAVE CHOSEN NOT TO SEEK SERVICES

Students may not feel comfortable seeking services for various reasons. You may be concerned that accepting accommodations means that you're slacking or using a "crutch." On the contrary—seeking accommodations and using them means that you're aware that you need an extra boost. You wouldn't tell a person who is blind that being blind makes him a slacker!

Some students may be concerned about being "labeled." Others may have philosophical or moral objections to ADD being seen as a disability. However, ADD has been legally classified as a disability. That means that ADD has an impact on your day-to-day living, particularly your academic performance. Classifying ADD as a disability doesn't change the fact that people with ADD have many positive qualities. It's a classification system—nothing more, nothing less. Labels aren't bad; they just are.

If you're concerned that information regarding your ADD will be disclosed to others without your permission at some point in the future, know that there are strict laws in place that govern the confidentiality of your diagnosis and services through the school.

If you don't apply for services now, you can always change your mind and apply later. However, keep in mind that the review process takes time—during which you will continue to attend classes, work on research papers, take exams, and receive grades (which cannot be changed), all without any accommodations. Certainly, in the absence of formal accommodations, you can always ask professors if they would mind giving you extra time on a test or let you record a lecture. If they say no, however, you have no further avenues to take, and you may have to struggle through that test without help.

In this chapter, you learned about your rights as a registered disabled student and the OSDS required evaluation. In the next chapter, you will learn about full psychiatric evaluations for ADD. You'll also learn about medications for ADD and the special issues faced by college students who take medication.

6

ADD and Medication

Being a college student living on your own is challenging enough. But, as a person with ADD, you may have the additional responsibility of managing your medication. In this chapter, you'll learn how to best handle this issue.

DO YOU NEED MEDICATION?

You may be wary of taking medication for ADD. This is understandable. However, although it may seem as though too many people are needlessly taking ADD medications, scientific studies demonstrate that 75 percent of adults with ADD are undiagnosed, and that only 11 percent of adults with ADD take medication (Kessler et al. 2006). Despite these statistics, and the reports in the media, medications do help, and you should consider seeking an evaluation for medication as part of your overall ADD treatment plan.

Medications Can Help You Succeed in College

Look at it this way: Going to college with ADD is like climbing the Himalayas with a backpack full of rocks. You could make it to the top of the mountain (graduation day), but it's going to take a lot more energy and time than it would if you didn't have all those rocks. Medication helps get some of the rocks out of the backpack. Although it doesn't get rid of all of them, it can greatly reduce the burden as you continue to climb that mountain.

Medications Decrease Substance Abuse

People with ADD have a low level of a brain chemical called dopamine. When you have a low level of dopamine (as is the case with people with untreated ADD), you will find ways to raise that level. Some people find relief from their ADD by abusing illicit drugs. You may be concerned you'll become addicted to your stimulant medication, or you may have been told that you're just taking "speed." However, if you take medication for ADD, your dopamine level rises, resulting in a decrease of ADD symptoms. You no longer need to seek illicit drugs to make your brain feel like it's not afflicted with ADD. In fact, people with ADD who do not take medication for it are four times more likely to abuse substances than people who are treated (Biederman 2003).

The reason some people have gotten addicted to stimulants is that they are seeking a side effect—for example, losing weight or staying up without needing sleep. People quickly become tolerant of the side effects and need higher and higher doses of stimulants to achieve their goal. In major contrast, the benefits of improving attention and decreasing distractibility are maintained at the same therapeutic dose.

Do You Need Medication?

You may be struggling to decide whether you really need additional things like medication to help you through college (and life). Here are some questions to ask yourself.

1. Do you find that you have to work twice as hard as your classmates but still don't seem to get the same grades?

2. Do you feel that you are a chronic underachiever and you just haven't worked to your potential?

3. Have you injured yourself due to inattention or impulsive or daredevil behavior?

4. Have you gotten into legal trouble due to your impulsivity?

5. Have you tried different study techniques and nothing seems to be working?

6. Do you have family members with ADD who have received positive results from medication?

7. Does your excessive talking or interrupting strain your relationships?

8. Do you have a hot temper or short fuse?

9. Have you lost jobs or quit because you were bored or impulsive?

10. Do you lack confidence in your abilities because of past failures?

11. Have your friends or family members made comments about your behavior or lack of follow-through?

It's important to show this list of questions to your friends and family and ask them their opinions, since people with ADD can have difficulties evaluating the severity of their behavior. The more questions you answered with a yes, the more you may benefit from ADD medication treatment. Later in this chapter, we'll discuss the various medications prescribed for ADD.

EVALUATIONS

Usually you will receive an evaluation from a qualified clinician before you are prescribed medication. An evaluation for medication may be more detailed than the kind of evaluation you receive for special school accommodations, which we covered in chapter 5. Clinicians who may specialize in ADD include psychiatrists, nurse practitioners, physician assistants, mental health counselors, psychologists, or clinical social workers. When making an appointment, ask what experience the clinician has had treating people with ADD. Be aware that only physicians (including psychiatrists), nurse practitioners, and physician assistants can prescribe medication. If the health care provider does not prescribe medication, find out about his or her attitudes regarding medication for ADD. Make sure the provider's philosophy is in line with yours.

Paying for Evaluations

Like many college students, you may be on a limited income, so finding the funds to pay for an evaluation can be a challenge. Check with your medical insurance company to see if they cover evaluations. You may want to check with the health care provider to see if they accept patients on a "sliding scale"; this means that the provider bases the fee on your income. You can also ask your parents if they can loan you money for an evaluation or simply cover the expense. Explain to them that an evaluation may help you receive medication and/or accommodations that can help you succeed in school.

Bring a Family Member to Your Appointment

People with ADD have a difficult time observing and accurately reporting their own behavior. It helps to bring a family member with you, particularly a parent, because he may give a more accurate representation of your symptoms and how they affect your functioning. It's also important to have a family member at your appointment so he or she can help you give a full family history to the doctor. Your mom and dad probably know more about their parents' ADD, depression, and anxiety symptoms than you do.

Preparing for Your Evaluation Appointment

A specialist will ask about your family history of ADD and other disorders. By finding out who else in your family has had ADD, depression, or anxiety, the evaluator will be better able to determine what might be going on with you. The evaluator will also ask what you were like as a child—if you got into a lot of accidents, daydreamed, or engaged in "daredevil" behavior. In addition, you may be asked to fill out some ADD symptom questionnaires and/or take a computer game or test that measures your rate of impulsivity and distractibility.

Frequently Asked Questions

Here are a few questions the evaluator may ask you:

- How long have you had problems paying attention?

- Do you put off things until the last minute?

- Do you have difficulty getting organized and staying organized?

- Do you have a history of drug, alcohol, or tobacco use?

- Have you ever been arrested?

- Do you have a hard time staying in your seat for long periods of time?

- Do you have any feelings of internal restlessness?

- Do you have difficulty making friends?

- How many jobs have you had in the past year?

- How many speeding tickets do you have?

- How are you with standing in line or waiting in traffic?

- Is there anyone in your family who has been diagnosed with ADD or you suspect has ADD?

- Have you ever been hit on the head or knocked out?

- Are you allergic to any medications?

Write the answers to these questions in a notebook before you go to your appointment. That way you can make sure you don't leave any information out. During the appointment, if the doctor asks you a question that you don't understand, don't feel comfortable with, or don't know how to answer, let the doctor know. A simple "I don't understand" or "I don't know" will suffice.

Bring the following materials to your appointment: your medical insurance card; driver's license or state-issued photo ID; report cards and behavior reports from elementary, middle, and high school; and transcripts from your college.

Working with Your Doctor

"Working with your doctor" doesn't mean that you bring him to your job at the campus bookstore. It means having a doctor with whom you feel comfortable and can openly discuss information about your health. The more comfortable you are talking to your doctor, the more likely you'll be to show up for appointments and take his or her advice.

SHOULD YOU GET A DOCTOR CLOSER TO SCHOOL?

You may already have a doctor in your hometown who prescribes medication for ADD. Some college students choose to keep their doctor and go to medical appointments when they're home for spring or winter break. Others feel more comfortable having a doctor nearby, knowing that the doctor is more accessible to them if there is an unexpected problem with their medication.

If you want to find a doctor in your college town, talk to your regular doctor about practitioners he would recommend. It's okay to let your doctor know you'd like to see someone closer to you—it will show that you're taking more responsibility for your health care. Plus, giving referrals is part of your doctor's job. You can also ask a trusted friend or relative who has experience with ADD for a referral.

Should You Get a Doctor in Your College Town?

Ask yourself the following questions:

- Have you started a new medication or dosage recently?

- Do you have anxiety and/or depression along with your ADD?

- Did your hometown doctor recommend that you see a doctor near you?

- Are you planning on staying in town after you graduate?

- Is there an ADD specialist in your new town?

The more questions you answered with a yes, the more you should consider getting a doctor in your new town.

BE HONEST WITH THE DOCTOR

It's very important that you don't keep information from your doctor. Your doctor has seen it and heard it all, so you aren't going to shock anyone. Telling the truth can save you from complications and side effects. If you feel uncomfortable with one doctor, you can always switch to another.

KEEPING APPOINTMENTS

Be careful—some doctor's offices charge you a fee if you don't show up for an appointment, and some offices have you reschedule if you're more than fifteen minutes late. In addition, many doctors will not refill your prescription until you reschedule and attend your next appointment. Ask the doctor's front desk staff to mail you a reminder card and call you the day before your appointment to remind you, if possible.

I write things down, like filling in my own appointment card at the doctor's office. This way I will never forget. If I have written it down, it is permanently stored in my memory.
—Courtney, sophomore, Santa Fe Community College

UNDERSTANDING ADD MEDICATION

If you took medication for your ADD when you were a child, you may remember having to leave class and go to the school nurse to get your second dose of medicine for the day. The most commonly prescribed medications for ADD are now in long-acting or *extended release* form. This means that you take one pill in the morning and it lasts most or all of the day.

You may have stopped taking medication because you felt that it didn't work, was too time consuming, or made you feel different from your usual self. You are not alone. In a recent study (Wolraich et al. 2005), 68 percent of fifteen-year-olds reported that they had stopped taking their medication. You may have avoided taking medication because you worried about the potential for addiction. However, there are now additional medication options available to you, so you may be able to find a medication that does a better job of meeting your needs.

The two types or classes of medication now approved by the U.S. Food and Drug Administration (FDA) for the treatment of ADD are stimulants and nonstimulants. Strattera (atomoxetine) is the only nonstimulant approved for ADD. There are also new forms of medication. For instance, a skin patch, Daytrana (methylphenidate transdermal system), has been developed as a convenient method of delivering ADD medication. Even if a medication is not approved by the FDA for the treatment of ADD, your doctor can still prescribe it. An FDA approval simply means that the medication can be advertised by the pharmaceutical company as a treatment for a particular disorder, but certain other medications have benefits for people with ADD and can be prescribed by a physician, at his or her discretion.

Types of Medication

As mentioned above, a variety of medications may be prescribed for the treatment of ADD. Keep in mind that you may need to be patient as your doctor tries to find the optimal medication and dose. Unlike other disorders, there is no blood test for ADD, and not all medications affect everyone in the same way, so finding a medication and dose that works can take trial and error.

STIMULANTS

Stimulants increase attention, decrease hyperactivity, and decrease impulsivity by stimulating the frontal lobes of the brain. Methylphenidate and amphetamines are the only prescribed stimulants. The most noticeable side effects of stimulants are decreased appetite, headaches, and difficulty sleeping. In rare cases, people may develop tics (involuntary movements) after taking stimulants.

Stimulants are classified as "Schedule II" medications by the FDA. This means that they are considered "controlled substances," medications that have an addictive potential. Some people abuse stimulants for their side effects, such as increased alertness and weight loss. Because of the potential for abuse, prescriptions for stimulant medications cannot be called in to a pharmacy by your doctor—you have to pick up the prescription at the doctor's office and bring it to the pharmacy to be filled.

Extended-release stimulants, such as Concerta, Vyvanse, Daytrana, Focalin XR, Adderall XR, and Dexedrine spansules, last from eight to twelve hours, making it more convenient to take the medications, and allowing for a more continuous delivery of the medication. Extended-release stimulants allow you to take your medication first thing in the morning, rather than at two different times during the day, as you might with immediate-release stimulants, such as Ritalin, Focalin, and Dexedrine, which last three to four hours.

Stimulant overdosing. When you have ADD, your brain produces a low level of the neurotransmitter dopamine. When you take ADD medication as prescribed, the level of dopamine in your brain goes up to a normal level, that of a person without ADD. But when you take too much stimulant medication, either by accident or with the purpose of trying to get high, you are pushing your dopamine up to a level that is way too high for your brain to handle. Overdosing on stimulants can give you unpleasant experiences such as tactile hallucinations and insomnia. With a tactile hallucination, you feel things that aren't there, such as the sensation of bugs crawling on or inside your skin. Not very pleasant. Obviously, it's a bad idea to take more medication than has been prescribed to you.

Rebound. This kind of rebound is different from the ones that have to do with basketball or a failed relationship. It's what can happen when your stimulant medication wears off. You may notice that you have a temporary increase in frustration or ADD symptoms around the time that your stimulant medication wears off in the afternoon. The phenomenon of your ADD temporarily seeming worse is called *rebound*. Some people use an immediate-release stimulant for studying in the early evening, after their extended-release medication has worn off. Discuss your specific needs with your doctor.

Drug testing and stimulant medication. If you are taking stimulant medication, your urine will show up positive for amphetamines on drug tests, even if you stop taking your stimulant medication prior to the test. If your college does random drug testing, carry a signed note from your doctor stating the name of your medication, the fact that it's a stimulant, that you are prescribed the medication for ADD, and that a drug test could show a positive result for amphetamines. If you live off campus and need to take a dose of your medication while you are on campus, bring a small amount of your medication with you in the original labeled pill bottle. (You can ask the pharmacy to split your medication between two bottles so you can keep the rest in a pill bottle at home.) If you're traveling, remember to bring the original bottle and a letter from your doctor. If you're applying for a job that requires a drug test, let your prospective employer know ahead of time that you take stimulant medication for ADD and that it may show up positive on the test.

According to the guidelines of the National Collegiate Athletic Association (NCAA), medications for ADD are acceptable. The yearly NCAA drug testing does not check for stimulants, but the drug testing done around the NCAA championship games does check for stimulants. If you're an athlete, make sure that you provide your team physician or coach with a letter from your doctor regarding your prescription. In cases where an athlete's drug test comes back positive for amphetamines, the university submits medical documents to the NCAA—but the university needs to have those documents ahead of time in order to submit them!

NONSTIMULANTS

If you took ADD medication as a kid (or even if you take it now), it most likely came from the stimulant category. However, nonstimulants have also been found to help diminish ADD symptoms. There are currently two main nonstimulants that are prescribed for ADD—Strattera and Wellbutrin.

Strattera. In 2002, Strattera became the first nonstimulant approved by the FDA for the treatment of ADD, and the first medication approved for adult ADD. Strattera is different from a stimulant in that it is chemically more like an antidepressant. This medication is included in the class of drugs called selective norepinephrine reuptake inhibitors (SNRIs), which allow more norepinephrine (a neurotransmitter) to hang out in the spaces between neurons. SNRIs also increase the amount of dopamine in the prefrontal cortex of the brain. This increase in norepinephrine and dopamine helps increase alertness and the ability to focus. The most common side effects are stomach upset and dry mouth. Strattera is not addictive, so it's not a Schedule II drug.

Wellbutrin. Wellbutrin (bupropion) is a norepinephrine and dopamine reuptake inhibitor (NDRI). Like Strattera, this medication allows more norepinephrine to linger between the neurons, but it allows dopamine to share that space as well. Wellbutrin is indicated by the FDA for depression and not for ADD, but it has shown promise in helping to reduce ADD symptoms in young adults (Solhkhah et al. 2005). A common side effect is dry mouth. In rare cases, seizures may occur, particularly in people who have a history of anorexia or bulimia. An overdose of Wellbutrin can cause tremors and seizures.

The Deal with Side Effects

You may be concerned about potential side effects from your medication. To put this in perspective, remember that any behavior has side effects, both pleasant and unpleasant.

The decision to take or not take medication boils down to an evaluation of the risks and benefits. The benefits of medication, such as being able to focus more effectively when studying and getting higher grades, may outweigh the occasional tiredness or disorganization you feel when your medication wears off. Also, the fact that you're experiencing a side effect doesn't mean you have to live with it. Although a side effect like dry mouth may be hard to eliminate, other side effects, such as jitteriness or insomnia, should be easy to eliminate with a change of dosage or medication.

To view this from a broader perspective, look at the side effects on a bottle of aspirin. Pretty scary, huh? And this is a medication that's used by millions of people a day. Here's one reason for all those scary side effects reported on the bottle: When drug companies do clinical trials to get their medications approved by the FDA, they need to report any medical event that occurs during the trial. So even if a participant falls off a bar stool and gets a bruise on her side while taking the drug being studied, bruising has to be recorded as a possible side effect, no matter how unlikely it is that the bruise was actually a result of the medication.

WHEN TO CALL YOUR DOCTOR

It's definitely wise to take side effects seriously, however. If you have any physical or emotional reactions that are out of the range of your normal behavior, are causing you difficulty in functioning, or are different from the side effects listed for the medication, contact your doctor.

Sometimes people feel that they're bothering their doctor by reporting problems with their medication. In fact, the opposite is true. Even if the problem is minor, the doctor would rather find out now that you're having a problem with the medicine than at your next appointment, a few months later. This is where having a doctor in your town helps—you can see him or her right away if you're having any concerns.

KEEP A MEDICATION LOG

If you're already taking medication, it's helpful to keep a log of what time you took your medication, any side effects you noticed, and information about what has or hasn't changed for you. For example, you may not argue as much with people or bite your fingernails quite as often, or you might notice that you've been having hand tremors. Having everything written down can make your medical appointments more beneficial and efficient, both for you and your doctor. Make copies of the Medication Log on the next page and fill it out daily. Take the copies to your next doctor's appointment.

Medication Compliance

Because a symptom of ADD is forgetfulness, it can be difficult to remember to take your medication every day. A useful tool is a pill organizer that is labeled with the days of the week, which you refill every Sunday, for example. If you forget whether you've taken your medication on a particular day, all you have to do is check the container for that day. This also helps eliminate double dosing.

Another way to remember to take your medication is to take it at the same time every day. Set an alarm on your cell phone and clock to remind you. By taking your medication at the same time, you develop a routine, and you also ensure that your medication is evenly dosed in your body.

A study found that 22 percent of people with ADD either took too much or misused their medication (Wilens et al. 2006). It's not surprising that the more severe your ADD symptoms, the less likely you are to take your medication regularly (Safren et al. 2007). When you have ADD,

Medication Log

Date: _____

Time took medicine: _____ A.M. P.M. (Circle one.)

Today's events:

_____

_____

_____

Side effects and how they affected my functioning:

_____

_____

_____

it can be easy to forget to take your medication or take more than the prescribed amount in order to focus for longer periods of time. Luckily, the more insight you gain into your ADD (by reading this book, among other things), the more likely you are to take your medication as it is prescribed. You are also more likely to take your medication if you are seeing benefits and have a low rate of side effects. This is why it's important to tell your doctor how your medication is affecting you. There are several different medications available, and if one is causing problems for you another might work better.

> I keep my pill organizer next to my toothbrush. That makes it easy
> to remember.
>
> —Bailey, junior, Winthrop University

Take Your Medication with Food

It's important to have food in your stomach when you take your medication, unless you have been directed otherwise by your doctor or pharmacist. Even if you're not a breakfast eater, it is highly recommended that you get some kind of coating in your stomach before taking your medication, to decrease the chances of stomach upset. Peanut butter and milk are good for keeping your stomach coated and happy. Even a breakfast shake may be enough to keep your stomach satisfied.

Refrain from washing your medication down with a citrus drink, such as grapefruit or orange juice. Citrus drinks can change the potency of some medications, so it's best to just wash your pill down with water.

Use of Alcohol and Medication

A few people may react poorly to mixing medications and alcohol. If you drink while taking a stimulant medication, you may not experience the usual effect of your alcohol intake, and you may drink more than you are used to. When the stimulant medication wears off, you may suddenly feel the full effects of the alcohol you have ingested; you may feel quite intoxicated and ill. Also, keep in mind that even if you don't feel a buzz because you're taking stimulant medication, alcohol will still impair your reflexes. If you start a new medication, be very careful about alcohol consumption until you are knowledgeable about how that combination affects you, and remember that everyone may have a different reaction.

Medication Changes

Depending on how you feel and function while taking your medication, your doctor may want to change your medication or dosage periodically. Because there are no blood tests for ADD, your doctor may have to adjust your medications or dosage to find what works best for you. That is why it's important that you are specific with your doctor about how you are feeling and whether there is any difference in your academic performance or relationships.

MED HOLIDAYS

Some people decide to not take their stimulant medication on weekends, or during periods when they don't have classes. However, since ADD affects all aspects of life, it is recommended that you do not take "med holidays." You may find that your medication has not only improved your academic performance but also helped with your relationships, so it's best to keep taking it on a daily basis.

Be aware that you can skip taking stimulants for a day, if necessary, but the nonstimulants—Strattera and Wellbutrin—build up gradually and must be taken every day.

Clinical Trials

Clinical trials are where drugs are tested, part of the process for approval by the FDA. You may notice ads in the college newspaper, on the radio, and on TV for clinical trials involving patients with ADD. If you were to participate in a clinical trial, you'd be given assessment tests to track your progress and you'd receive the study drug. You would also meet with the study physician at every visit.

Advantages of participating in clinical trials include receiving the study medication at a low cost or at no cost, having an extensive assessment, seeing a specialized study physician at every visit, possibly receiving payment for your participation, and having access to treatment that otherwise wouldn't be available to you. In addition to meeting with a physician, you may also meet with other specialists. Plus, physicians who are chosen to conduct clinical trials for ADD drugs have often been recognized as experts in the field.

Disadvantages include possibly having to discontinue some of your other medications, attending more frequent appointments than you would have with your regular doctor, and the need to meet strict requirements in order to be included in the study.

Abuse of ADD Medication on Campus

It can be tempting to sell your medication—it's a quick way to make money, and you have the medication available. Approximately 26 percent of adolescents who are prescribed stimulant medication for ADD sell or give away their medication (Poulin 2007). Don't do this! Most colleges have strict drug policies that include mandatory disciplinary hearings. Some colleges even automatically expel students caught selling drugs. In addition, you can be prosecuted for a criminal offense. It doesn't matter if you are selling cocaine or selling your prescription medication—it is illegal either way. Any money you made from selling your medication would have to go right to your legal fees, and you might have difficulty getting accepted to another college with a record of an expulsion or suspension for selling drugs. And, for the rest of your life, you would have to check that little box on job and school applications next to the question "Have you ever been convicted . . ." *It is not worth it.*

Your friends may ask you if they can have a couple of pills because they have a big test or project due the next day and need to stay up. Just don't go there. Even if you aren't selling your medication, it's still not okay to give it to people. Medication affects everyone differently—each person's body chemistry is unique. Giving someone one of your pills, even with good intentions, can have disastrous results. If a friend takes one of your pills and dies, you could be charged with involuntary manslaughter. In a survey of over nine thousand undergraduates, it was found that 8.1 percent had used stimulant medication illicitly (McCabe, Teter, and Boyd 2006). That's a large group of young people putting themselves at risk unnecessarily. Protect yourself, and don't let your friends risk their health.

OTHER TREATMENTS

Available treatments for ADD extend beyond prescription medication. Currently, there is plenty of scientific evidence of the effectiveness of prescription medication, but more and more research is also being conducted on alternative treatments.

Herbals and Nutraceuticals

Unfortunately, there is little scientific evidence that these are effective in treating ADD. However, if you do choose to take any herbal supplements or nutraceutical drugs, make sure you tell your doctor, since some herbal preparations interact with the nervous system and/or your medication. Plus, herbals and nutraceuticals are not regulated by the FDA, so, unless the manufacturer adheres to strict quality assurance practices, you may be receiving different doses in each capsule (Curtis and Gaylord 2005).

Omega-3

There is evidence that omega-3 can help improve the symptoms of ADD. One study found that people with ADD had a significantly lower level of omega-3 fatty acids in their blood (Antalis et al. 2006). Fish oil and polyunsaturated fatty acids, which contain omega-3 and omega-6, have been found to increase this level (Sinn and Bryan 2007; Young, Conquer, and Thomas 2005).

In this chapter, you learned about the medications available for the treatment of ADD, and the risks and benefits of those medications. Medication is just one of the ways you can take better care of yourself. In the next chapter, you will learn more about wellness and self-care.

7

Live Well and Prosper

It's normal for young people to embark on a process of "finding themselves" while in college. However, this process can seem exaggerated when you have ADD. If you have ADD, you're more likely to have mood swings, take things to extremes, and have a high level of frustration. As a result, keeping yourself on an even keel may be more of a challenge. This is why it's important to learn how to practice good self-care and maintain wellness. Wellness encompasses several different aspects of life: good nutrition, physical fitness and exercise, adequate sleep, emotional stability, and healthy relationships. Protecting your wellness in all of these areas is called "self-care." This is very important for people with ADD to learn because people who are impulsive and distractible can easily forget to pay attention to their basic needs.

College is a high-stress environment. You're experiencing pressure to get good grades, make social connections, and still maintain your relationships with people at home. You may find that, due to your ADD, you have to work twice as hard to get the same amount of work done as everyone else, and your frustration level can go through the roof. During high school, your parents might have been around to let you know when you needed a break from studying. Now you need to monitor yourself, and that can be tricky. Why? Sometimes people with ADD don't take care of themselves because they think it means slowing down—and since they know how much effort it takes to make any progress, they don't want to lose ground by taking time away from working. However, taking care of yourself doesn't mean that you need to move at a snail's pace. You can take care of yourself and still have an active, productive lifestyle.

> *Get on a regular sleep schedule. Nothing helps ADD like a good night's sleep. Something that will help you achieve a good night's sleep is exercise. Going to the gym three to five times a week helps me to get regular sleep and keeps me from getting antsy in class.*
> —Todd, junior, University of Florida

WELLNESS ISSUES COMMON TO PEOPLE WITH ADD

Particular health and wellness issues appear more frequently in the lives of people with ADD—stress, Internet addiction, problems with managing anger, depression, anxiety, suicide, drug and alcohol addiction, and eating disorders. This doesn't mean that other people don't experience these issues. It's just that people with ADD are more likely to deal with these difficulties, and their experiences can be more intense.

Stress

People with ADD have a tendency to get more worked up about things than others do. For this reason, it's important that you stick to a stress relief practice. What do you like to do for fun or to relax? Listen to music, watch a movie? Make sure you incorporate fun activities into your schedule. You don't necessarily have to be still in order to relax—you can continue to move around and do things while still having the benefits of relaxation.

Massage can be very beneficial. See if there's a massage school in the area that offers massages for a reduced rate. You may be concerned that you cannot lie still long enough for a massage, but you may find that it relaxes you so much that you wouldn't even consider moving. You can also ask for a thirty-minute massage instead of an hour.

People with ADD can experience deep relaxation from guided imagery, in which you might listen to a CD of a person describing relaxing scenes. Since the ADD mind is creative, imagery (visualization) provides your brain with stimulating input while helping you relax at the same time.

Television and Internet Use

People with ADD are more likely to become addicted to the Internet (Yen et al. 2007). There's just so much distracting content out there! So, when you want to use the Internet for purely social or leisure reasons, set a kitchen timer for thirty minutes. When the timer goes off, stop using the computer. You may even need to completely shut down the computer so you aren't tempted to start using it again. Also, pay attention to your behavior when you're doing academic research or taking an online class—as you undoubtedly know, it can be so easy to veer off and start surfing the Internet for fun.

Frequent television use has been associated with weight gain (Parsons, Manor, and Power 2007). In addition, people who watch traumatic events repeatedly on television can develop nightmares and trauma-related anxiety (Propper et al. 2007). Put strict limits on your television use and turn off the television at least one hour before you go to bed. Besides, you're supposed to be studying, remember?

Anger Management

People with ADD can have a difficult time managing their anger. Because of impulsivity, you may not have any built-in reaction time, during which most people might think about their response before acting. You may not have the ability to pause and talk yourself down from a potential blowup. In addition, impulsivity plus anger can make you ten times as distractible. This tendency can affect your academic performance and your relationships. Medication can give you the extra time you need to calm down before you do or say something problematic.

Be aware of how your body reacts to anger. You may notice that when you get angry your hands tremble or shake, your face feels flushed, you clench your teeth, and your heart beats more rapidly. The key to maintaining control is to notice when your anger starts ramping up and cut it off at the pass. Walk away from the situation—you can always come back and talk about it after you've calmed down. For most people, the trick of counting to ten as a method of calming down may work just fine—but if you have ADD, increase that number to twenty-five. In chapter 9, you'll learn about other effective ways to handle irritating situations.

Depression and Anxiety

About 25 to 50 percent of people with ADD also have difficulties with depression or anxiety (Fischer, Bau, et al. 2007). Keep in mind that depression and anxiety can look very similar: you may worry a lot or become teary for no reason, or life may seem like it is spiraling out of control. To find out whether you might be experiencing either of these conditions, take a look at the checklist below.

Do You Have Depression or Anxiety?

Check off the boxes next to the statements that apply to you. Pay particular attention to how you've felt in the past month.

☐ Not enjoying your favorite activities like you used to (This is different from boredom.)

☐ Having crying spells or feeling teary

☐ Withdrawing from social activities

☐ Having trouble being cheered up

☐ Dreading getting up in the morning

☐ Feeling panicked for no reason

☐ Fearing going out in public

☐ Being easily irritated

☐ Gaining or losing significant amounts of weight

☐ Having difficulty sleeping

☐ Experiencing increased worrying

☐ Waking up too early in the morning and not being able to get back to sleep

☐ Pacing or hand-wringing

☐ Moving or talking slower than normal

☐ Feeling like you'd be better off dead or wishing you could disappear

If you checked off two or more of these boxes, or if you have any feelings of not wanting to be around anymore, contact a mental health professional for help.

Treatment is available, but if you're in the throes of depression and anxiety, it can be difficult to summon the energy to get help. In a study of almost three thousand college students, only 36 percent who met diagnostic criteria for depression sought medication or counseling treatment (Eisenberg, Golberstein, and Gollust 2007). If your depression or anxiety has become debilitating, you may want to consider asking a friend or family member to make an appointment for you with a mental health clinician, and have them take you to the appointment. Counseling and medication can help you start feeling like you are part of life again. In severe cases, feelings of depression and anxiety can lead a person into the territory of self-harm. This is when suicide becomes an issue.

SUICIDE

Some people with ADD find that the pressures of college are too much to bear. Suicide is the second-leading cause of death among college students. From 1990 to 2004, the rate of suicide across college campuses was 6.5 students per 100,000 (Schwartz 2006). And people with ADD are more prone to depression and suicide than are people without ADD.

If you have thoughts of hurting yourself or feel that you'd be better off dead, call the college's crisis phone number, or call the National Suicide Prevention Lifeline (listed in the Resources section of this book). You can find the phone numbers for your local services inside the front cover of your phone book. Be aware that if the police or crisis center staff members feel that you're a danger to yourself or others, they may involuntarily hospitalize you. But the alternative—hurting yourself—is far worse.

Drug and Alcohol Use

One of the reasons you have ADD is that you have a low level of the brain chemical dopamine. And if your brain is missing a chemical, it will find a way to get it, whether it's through prescribed, helpful medication or through illegal substances. (Remember, people with ADD who take prescribed medication are much less likely to abuse illicit drugs [Faraone et al. 2007].)

One in five ADD adults has experienced substance abuse (Wilens and Upadhyaya 2007). People with ADD are more likely to abuse alcohol and drugs, including nicotine and caffeine. They start using drugs at an earlier age and experience more intense use than people without ADD do (Wilens et al. 2005). Approximately 35 to 71 percent of alcoholics have ADD (Wilens 2004). And there's a much higher rate of ADD among addicts than there is in the general population (Wilens et al. 2006).

People with ADD are more likely to succumb to peer pressure. If you've ever felt like you just don't fit in, then you know that being passed a joint at a party can seem like an invitation to join the group. Many people who are addicted say that they originally started using drugs and alcohol in order to feel calmer in social situations. So you can see how people with ADD would be especially prone to falling into this trap.

Let's say you've realized you have a problem with drugs or alcohol. What do you do? First, contact the doctor who prescribed your ADD medication, if you're taking any, and tell him or her about your drug and alcohol use. It's important that you report what you are using, how much you are using, and how often you use it, since your prescribed medications may interact with your "self-medications." Next, think about whether you can fight your addiction on your own; you may want to consider taking time off of school and entering a treatment program. Be honest with yourself and others about your use.

Do You Need Treatment for Addiction?

Take the following quiz to determine if you need treatment for addiction.

- Do you need to use more and more of the substance to feel "high"?

- Do you hide your substance use?

- Are any of your friends substance users?

- Has your substance use caused any legal problems for you?

- Do you "black out" and have difficulty remembering events that happen when you're using?

- Have you lied or stolen in order to obtain the substance?

- Has your family showed concern over your substance use?

- Has your use (or hangover/withdrawal) affected your class or job attendance?

- Have you promised to quit but can't seem to do it?

If you answered yes to any of these questions, then you may have an addiction. Talk to a mental health professional about treatment options.

Keep in mind that, regardless of your ADD status, if you break a college's rule regarding alcohol or drug use, and you're under the age of twenty-one or if you are claimed as a dependent on your parents' income taxes, your parents may be informed of your infraction. This policy is covered under the federal law known as the Family Educational Rights and Privacy Act (FERPA).

IF YOU ARE IN RECOVERY

For anyone in recovery, college can present some temptations that are hard to avoid. People with ADD are even more likely to relapse into addiction (White et al. 2004). When you first arrive on campus, look up the college Alcoholics Anonymous (AA) or Narcotics Anonymous (NA) chapters and start going to meetings regularly. Remember, NA is open to all drug addicts. See the Resources section for contact information.

SPECIFIC DRUG ISSUES

People with ADD can be particularly susceptible to caffeine, nicotine, marijuana, and cocaine use and abuse. When you have ADD, not only is there an increased risk of addiction, but it is also more difficult to quit permanently. When your brain is low on a certain necessary chemical, such as dopamine in the case of ADD, you will find a way of replacing it, consciously or unconsciously. And it can be very difficult to overcome your brain's desire for that chemical.

Caffeine. Sometimes people with ADD consume large quantities of coffee or caffeinated soda. The truth is, caffeine *does* help you focus—but only for about a half hour. The side effects of caffeine, including stomachaches, irritable bowel problems, nervousness, and insomnia, last longer than the beneficial effects.

The side effects of caffeine withdrawal are pretty nasty—they can include headaches, nausea, and vomiting. If you plan on weaning yourself off of caffeine, it is recommended that you drink a little less each day (mixed with decaf, if you wish) instead of going cold turkey. This will help reduce withdrawal symptoms as you lessen your body's dependence on caffeine.

Nicotine. People with ADD start smoking at a younger age, smoke more cigarettes per day, and have a harder time quitting the habit than those without ADD. The more severe your ADD symptoms, the more likely it is that you'll be a regular smoker (Kollins, McClernon, and Fuemmeler 2005). Smokers with ADD also have a greater risk of using other drugs (Biederman et al. 2006). If you'd like to quit smoking, you might consider talking with your doctor about medications that might make it easier to quit, including Wellbutrin/Zyban (bupropion), Chantix (varenicline), and nicotine patches and gum.

Marijuana and cocaine. Some people with untreated ADD report that when they use marijuana or cocaine, it is the only time that their brain feels "normal." However, marijuana use has negative side effects, such as the loss of short-term memory and lack of motivation, and cocaine has a side effect of agitation. Both of these drugs come with the risk of addiction, and they're illegal. If you already have ADD, you really can't spare any short-term memory or mood stability. Medication treatment for ADD can decrease the need for substance use (Levin et al. 2007) and can help your brain feel "normal," without all the negative side effects and the risk of jail time.

Eating Disorders

Just like drug and alcohol abuse, eating disorders are a type of addiction—one involving control. People with ADD may be prone to eating disorders because of the rush they get from denying themselves food or from bingeing. In one study, it was found that the rate of eating disorders (primarily binge eating) in an ADD adult population was the highest rate of any comorbid disorder (Mattos et al. 2004). Girls with ADD can be almost four times as likely to develop an eating disorder as non-ADD girls (Biederman et al. 2007). Some people with ADD may find that they focus better when they are starving, because their feeling of starvation provides them with a "concentrated distraction." Women especially may develop an eating disorder if they gain the "freshman fifteen." (Many students gain weight during their freshman year of college).

If you are bulimic (making yourself throw up or use laxatives after eating a large amount of food) or anorexic (restricting food), make sure you tell your doctor—medications such as Wellbutrin (bupropion) are not recommended for people with eating disorders since these disorders can increase the risk of seizure as a medication side effect.

Symptoms of Eating Disorders

If you (or a friend or roommate) have any of the following symptoms, this may be a sign of an eating disorder. Check off the boxes of the signs that apply:

☐ Secretive eating

☐ Hiding food

☐ Gaunt frame and hollow cheekbones

☐ Baggy clothes

☐ Dramatic weight loss in short period of time

☐ Eating large quantities of food in one sitting

☐ Use or hiding of laxatives or diet pills

☐ Perfectionistic personality

☐ Bruised or callused fingers/knuckles

☐ Loss of hair

☐ Grayish pallor of skin

The student health care center on campus may have a dietitian who specializes in eating disorders. If you feel that you might have an eating disorder, don't hesitate to ask for help, or at least to talk with someone at the health care center.

Beware of websites that actually promote eating disorders. These "pro-ana" and "pro-mia" sites should be avoided. For additional help with eating disorders, see the Resources section at the end of this book.

MAINTAINING YOUR PHYSICAL WELLNESS

If I knew I was going to live this long, I'd have taken better care of myself.

—Mickey Mantle

The better care you take of your body, the more effective you'll be in college. And that body will be with you for the rest of your life, so if you haven't been taking good care of it, now is the time to start.

Sleep well, eat well, and exercise. When you choose to ignore your body's needs, it is way easier to get distracted. I find when I meet these needs, I am happy, stay more positive, and am more motivated to concentrate even though it's a little harder for me to do that than other students.

—Shoshanna, junior, Penn State

Be Aware of What Your Body Is Telling You

People with ADD have problems paying attention not only to what is going on around them but also to what is going on with their own bodies. You don't realize you need to eat until your stomach is totally empty and growling. You may also hold a full bladder because you get so hyperfocused when you're doing something you enjoy. Check in with yourself often and see how you're doing. Are you tired? Hungry? Frustrated?

Listen to your body.

Health Insurance

Never go without health insurance. Without it, you'll pay much more in the long run—both in dollars and in the quality of your health. As mentioned earlier, people with ADD are much more prone to injury and accidents (in particular, head trauma and car accidents) than non-ADD people are (Sabuncuoglu 2007; Thompson et al. 2007), so health insurance is essential.

In most cases, you can continue to be covered on your parents' health insurance if you are under twenty-five and can provide the insurance company with proof that you're a full-time student. Check the policy to be sure. Colleges also have insurance plans at reduced rates for students. If you have this option at your college, choose the plan that covers doctors outside of the college, even if that plan is more expensive. It gives you more options in case you need specialized treatment.

On-Campus Health Care

Many college health care centers are more than just outpatient clinics. They may have travel immunization clinics, orthopedic specialists, flu shot clinics, pharmacies, and a host of other services. Some of the services are offered at a nominal fee or even for free for full-time students. Take advantage of these services, so that you can be as healthy as possible while in college.

Fighting the Freshman Fifteen

There are several reasons why it's easier for people with ADD to gain weight, and harder for them to take the weight off. People with ADD may eat because they're bored, or they eat without paying attention to what and how much they're eating. They also become bored and frustrated with diets. These tendencies only increase students' susceptibility to the dreaded "freshman fifteen"—the phenomenon in which college students (women, in particular) may gain up to fifteen pounds during their first year of college.

There are a few reasons for the freshman fifteen. You are now in charge of your own eating habits and are purchasing your own food. For budget reasons, you may be drawn to food that's less expensive, but less expensive food is often processed and isn't as healthy as fresh food. In addition, you may now have access to "all you can eat" dining halls, which can account for 20 percent of the "freshman fifteen" phenomenon (Levitsky, Halbmaier, and Mrdjenovic 2004).

Your schedule can also affect your eating habits. You may be more likely to eat on the run due to a calendar full of classes, social activities, study groups, and projects. You may also engage in the time-honored college tradition of ordering pizza with your friends at three in the morning. Snacking and eating junk food contributes to another 20 percent of the freshman fifteen (Levitsky, Halbmaier, and Mrdjenovic 2004).

Exercise and emotions also play a role in weight gain. You may not have the same exercise routine as before. You left your exercise partners back home, or maybe you played sports in high school and now don't have that outlet. And you most likely feel increased stress or homesickness and overeat as a result—eating carbohydrates increases the level of dopamine in the brain, which can temporarily relieve feelings of depression (Yeghiayan et al. 2004).

People with ADD also have a tendency to overeat because of inattention (Davis et al. 2006). They can hyperfocus on an activity, like watching TV, and suddenly realize they've eaten an entire bag of chips.

How can you prevent the freshman fifteen?

- Eat fresh food as much as possible. For example, eat a banana instead of a candy bar. Bananas are portable and come in their own packaging—a perfect snack.

- Eliminate refined sugar from your diet.

- Avoid "all you can eat" buffets.

- Stay away from "empty calories"—foods that have no nutritional content—like soft drinks.

- Don't skip meals.

- Eat slowly.

- Exercise on a daily basis.

- Always sit down to eat.

- Do not watch TV or read while eating—just focus on your meal.

Many campuses have dietitians on staff who can help you find healthy eating habits that are practical for a college lifestyle.

HEALTHY EATING

You may not be big on breakfast, but you should get something into your stomach in the morning, even if it's just a protein shake. You'll have more energy throughout the day and will be less likely to binge later. As you'll recall from chapter 6, eating breakfast also decreases the chances of having an upset stomach from your medication.

Always carry an energy bar or other high-protein snack with you. Put one in your backpack, one in your car, and one at your desk. Because of a difficulty with self-awareness, people with ADD may not realize they need food until they are ravenously hungry. And if you go too long without eating, your blood sugar level drops and you are at risk of passing out. Of course, even if you don't pass out, you're still not functioning at your best if your blood sugar level is low, so make an effort to eat at regular intervals throughout the day.

Exercise

As you read earlier, people with ADD have a low level of the brain chemical known as dopamine. Exercise can help raise that level, allowing you to focus better. Exercising for at least thirty minutes each day, first thing in the morning, will help you focus during the day.

People with ADD need variety in their exercise routine so they don't get bored. Look beyond traditional forms of exercise. Karate can help you find more self-discipline and has been successful for many people with ADD. Get involved in free intramural sports at your campus, or try something out of the ordinary, like fencing. Exercise need not be expensive. Your college may have a student fitness center that is free to full-time students and offers exercise equipment, classes, and lifestyle assessments—give it a try.

Exercise is a great way for me to release energy after a long day of classes. The discipline I learned in athletics carries over into my academics. It allows me to focus more on where the focus should be—on my studies.

—Jason, sophomore, University of Southern Maine

Finding Your Exercise Style

Once you get to college, it can be difficult getting into exercise mode. Since ADD is a motivation disorder, the inertia can really get to you. But, as you know, once you find something you enjoy, your focus can be laser sharp. Here's a quick quiz to help you find out what kind of exercise suits you best.

1. If I were on a treadmill at the gym, you would most likely find me

    a. Setting a goal for how far I could run

    b. Talking with the people around me

    c. Listening to a relaxation CD

    d. You wouldn't catch me anywhere near a treadmill.

2. What was your favorite activity in high school P.E.?

    a. Sprinting or racing against people

    b. Team sports, like volleyball

    c. Mental focus activities like yoga or karate

    d. Anything where I could watch instead of participating

3. I think exercise is

    a. A great way to challenge myself

    b. A great way to meet people

    c. A way to connect with my inner self

    d. Something I do only when I have to

4. I would most like to be known for

    a. My ability to achieve

    b. Being a good friend

    c. Having a deep connection to other living things

    d. Being aware of what is going on around me

If you answered with mostly *a*'s, you are a Competitor. You do best in activities where you get to show off your skills or you have a chance of besting a personal record. Look into competitive swimming, marathons, or running stadium steps.

If you answered with mostly *b*'s, you are a Socializer. You really enjoy being around other people when you exercise. Consider taking group fitness classes or participating in team sports such as volleyball or baseball.

If you answered with mostly *c*'s, you are an Intuitor. You like quieter activities that focus on the spiritual nature or interconnectedness of life. Look into yoga, tai chi, or karate.

If you answered with mostly *d*'s, you are an Observer. You like to participate in activities by watching them. Consider being a referee in an intramural sports team, or incorporate exercise into your already established routine. For example, if you take the bus, get off a couple of stops early and walk the extra blocks home.

Sleep Issues

The saying "an ounce of prevention is worth a pound of cure" definitely applies to sleep. Sleep deprivation makes it even harder for you to focus and keep your emotions in check. Sleep, on the other hand, is your body's built-in healer. Getting enough sleep is critical to your well-being and success. Unfortunately, college students with ADD are more likely to have sleep difficulties than their non-ADD peers are (Gau et al. 2007). And people with ADD have particular difficulty feeling refreshed upon waking up (Schredl, Alm, and Sobanski 2007).

GETTING ENOUGH SLEEP

The fact that you are able to stay up until four in the morning on the weekends doesn't mean you should. Throw roommates into the mix, and it can be even more difficult to get a good night's rest on a regular basis. However, try to get at least eight hours of sleep a night. You may be thinking, "Yeah, right. How am I ever going to get eight hours of sleep?" There will be times when you won't want to make yourself go to bed if it means missing out on social activities. When you have ADD, it's hard to see the long-term benefits of getting more sleep as your friends are going out for a night on the town. Keep in mind that sleep is your body's way of rejuvenating itself. The more sleep you get, the better equipped you'll be to handle life's challenges, and your focus (and grades) will improve.

Living with other people can increase the amount of noise filtering into your room, which can make it hard for you to fall asleep. Invest in some earplugs or noise-canceling headphones and play a relaxation CD or your favorite music as you go to sleep. Also, try to engage in a relaxing activity at least an hour before you go to bed.

If you do have an occasional late night, try to stick to your regular sleep schedule as closely as possible. For example, let's say you usually go to bed at 11:00 P.M. and get up at 8:00 A.M. However, Friday night you were out studying (well, that's the story you're sticking with, anyway) until 4:00 A.M. Try to get up as close to your normal waking time as possible on Saturday. The more you can stick to your regular waking time, the easier it will be to adjust when Monday comes around.

Many people with ADD are night owls—they work best when they stay up until the wee hours of the morning and then sleep until later in the day. If you're a night owl, make sure you schedule your classes for the afternoon hours and your study time for the evening, when you know your mind will be most alert. It may also help to find roommates who are also night owls, so you are all quiet at the same hours.

SLEEP DISORDERS

Some people with ADD grind their teeth while they're sleeping or when they're stressed or focusing. This problem is called *bruxism*. You can have your dentist fit you for a mouth guard that you wear at night. It may cost money to get a dental appliance like this, but it's worth it to protect your teeth. Untreated bruxism can lead to premature wearing down of your teeth and gums. You don't want worn-down teeth and receding gums when you're in your thirties or forties.

Sleep apnea is a serious sleep disorder in which your airway becomes blocked by the soft tissue in the back of your throat collapsing and closing. Snoring is a common symptom, and it is more common in people with ADD. Sleep apnea is a problem because it can regularly disrupt your sleep cycle. Even if you don't fully wake up when your airway is blocked, your brain may not be getting the sleep it needs, and this can result in even more problems paying attention (Beebe et al. 2004). You are also at risk for sleep apnea if you are overweight.

A test in a sleep lab can help determine if you have sleep apnea. The treatment for sleep apnea is a CPAP, a breathing machine that you wear at night. If you are having difficulties with tiredness that you can't explain, talk to your doctor about sleep apnea.

If insomnia is a problem for you, seek an evaluation from your doctor or a sleep specialist. Medications and supplements are available that can help you get a good night's rest. For example, melatonin is a supplement that has shown effectiveness in treating insomnia in people with ADD (Van der Heijden et al. 2007).

Keep a Sleep Log

Make a copy of this log and fill it out for a week. At the end of the week, review it and notice if there are any patterns. Did you feel more rested when you went to bed at 11:00 P.M. instead of 1:00 A.M., or did it not make much of a difference? Did you get a better night's sleep when you took your medication at 8:00 A.M. that morning instead of 10:00 A.M.? If you decide to see your doctor about your sleep difficulties, bring these logs with you. They can help you get the best treatment possible, which leads to increased zzzs.

Day of the week: _____

Date: _____

Time you took your medication: _____ A.M. P.M. (Circle one.)

Time you went to bed: _____ A.M. P.M.

Time you woke up: _____ A.M. P.M.

Number of times you woke up during the night: _____

How long were you up during the night (total)? _____ hours _____ minutes

How did you feel in the morning? (Circle one.)

Refreshed   Tired   Exhausted

What did you do during the hour before you went to bed?

_____

Safety and Prevention

While you're in college, you need to be extra careful about keeping safe. This means personal safety in addition to safety on the road—including knowing when you shouldn't get behind the wheel. This advice applies to everyone, but people with ADD must be especially careful, since they may be more likely to forget to lock their doors, not realize when they've had too much to drink, and get irate when they're cut off by someone on the road.

STAYING SAFE ON CAMPUS

Never walk alone at night. Always take someone with you. Many campuses have emergency call boxes that link you directly with the campus police. When you're in your apartment or dorm room, always keep the door locked. When you leave, make sure the doors and windows are all locked.

Having a security system for your house or apartment may help you feel more protected. However, you'll need to carry the code with you, since you may forget it and accidentally trigger the alarm. If your system is linked directly to the police, you can get fined for setting off the alarm in nonemergencies. You may want to consider not even setting it to save yourself the hassle. Sometimes just having a security system sticker in your window is enough of a burglar deterrent.

DAREDEVIL BEHAVIOR

People with ADD are more drawn to dangerous behavior—also known as "daredevil" behavior. Impulsivity, a tendency to get bored easily, and use of alcohol are often to blame for risky behaviors, such as "balcony surfing" (jumping from hotel balcony to hotel balcony), which can result in falls, traumatic brain injury, and death.

RAPE AND ITS CONNECTION TO ALCOHOL

Thirty-five out of every 1,000 college students are raped every year (Fisher, Cullen, and Turner 2000). Ninety percent of women involved in rapes know their assailants, and alcohol is a factor in half of those cases (Fisher, Cullen, and Turner 2000). Because increased alcohol consumption raises the risk of being a victim of rape, it's best to drink in moderation or, better yet, not drink at all (Parks and Fals-Stewart 2004). Avoiding alcohol is especially recommended for people with ADD, because they have a tendency to drink more than others, and medication can increase the effects of alcohol. If you're concerned that you won't blend in at a party if you don't have a drink in your hand, carry a glass or cup of club soda with you, or volunteer to be the designated driver. That will usually keep people from asking you why you aren't drinking.

SAFE DRIVING

Driving is an inherently risky activity, and safe driving is an important part of wellness. You may be driving much more than before, especially if you're attending college a far distance from home. The more severe the symptoms of ADD, the more likely a person will have a car accident, speeding ticket, or suspended license (Barkley 2006). Not only do people with ADD get into more car accidents, but they also sustain more damage to cars than non-ADD people (Fischer, Barkley, et al. 2007; Fried et al. 2006). Road tests show that young adults with ADD make more errors due to impulsivity, make more steering changes, and drive closer to the edges of roads than people without ADD (Fischer, Barkley, et al. 2007).

Here are some ways you can increase your safety while driving:

- Take your medication regularly. Studies show that stimulant medication can improve driving ability (Barkley, Murphy, et al. 2005).

- Get a manual transmission car. A study showed that people with ADD are safer drivers in stick-shift cars (Cox et al. 2006).

- Keep your radio at a very low volume or keep it off.

- Never talk on your cell phone while you're driving. Pull off to a safe, well-lit area if you *must* take a call.

- Make sure you are alert and calm before driving.

- Don't drive if you've been drinking.

- Drive during daylight hours whenever possible.

- Check all your tires before you drive.

- Regularly check the amount of fuel in your car.

Join an automobile association, which will provide maps, towing, and roadside assistance as part of your membership. Information on automobile assistance programs can be found in the Resources section at the end of this book. Keep an extra set of car keys in your home or dorm room and in your pocket or purse—it might save you from having to call the aforementioned automobile association when you lock yourself out of your car! (Some auto associations do have limits on the number of times you can call for free roadside assistance.)

If you're tempted to get a GPS unit for your car, think about it carefully first. Such a system can help you get to where you are going, but you may also be distracted by the screen. Another option is OnStar, where you can speak with an operator while you're driving.

Drunk driving. When ADD people and non-ADD people drink the same amount, the ADD person's driving performance is worse (Barkley et al. 2006). Only you can decide whether you are sober enough to drive home. Always keep some cash with you in case you need to get a cab; if you are ever in doubt of your ability to drive, get a ride home from a trusted friend or take a taxi. As you read in chapter 6, people with ADD can have a difficult time determining their level of impairment, especially if they are drinking while taking stimulant medication.

Road rage. College students with more severe ADD symptoms have higher rates of accidents related to anger while driving, and they engage in more aggressive and riskier driving behaviors while angry than do college students with less severe ADD. They also use ways of dealing with their anger that are less socially acceptable (Richards, Deffenbacher, and Rosen 2002). Since waiting in traffic can really ramp up an ADD person's anger and frustration, take alternate routes at times when you're likely to encounter traffic on main thoroughfares. Ask people who know the city well which shortcuts are best.

If you find yourself dealing with a slow or obnoxious driver, your car can feel like a pressure cooker. Play some soothing music and remind yourself that there have been times when you have also not driven to the best of your ability, and that you have even driven quite badly at times. We're all allowed to make mistakes. Take a deep breath and let it out slowly. You don't need to let this person ruin your day.

SEXUAL HEALTH

Young adults with ADD are more likely to engage in unprotected sex, have more sexual partners, and have more unplanned pregnancies. They are also more likely to contract a sexually transmitted disease (STD) than young adults without ADD are (Flory et al. 2006). Young adults with ADD have an STD rate of 16 percent, compared to 4 percent for non-ADD adults (Barkley, Fischer, et al. 2005).

If you're taking birth control pills, it can be difficult to remember to take your pill every day. Because of this, you may also want to consider birth control that requires less maintenance, such as Depo-Provera, a shot you receive every three months. However, because some STDs have no cure and can endanger your long-term health, insist on using a condom every time you have sex, limit your number of sexual partners, and get tested for STDs. Your college's health clinic may provide birth control at a lower cost, and they may also have a clinic for STD testing.

NURTURING YOUR SPIRITUAL AND EMOTIONAL WELLNESS

Taking care of your emotional and spiritual well-being is just as important as caring for your body and choosing safe behavior. Having spiritual beliefs means that you have a connection to something outside of yourself, whether it's a higher power or your community. Spirituality doesn't necessarily have anything to do with religion—you can be spiritual without going to a place of worship. However, going to a place of worship can help you find a community with common values. Since people with ADD can have a tendency to feel isolated or alone, it can be especially important for you to feel connected to others. If you feel so inclined, check out various spiritual communities and places of worship until you find one that feels right.

Seeking Outside Help

Sometimes, even with our best intentions, we still may need someone to help us out with the speed bumps in life. In addition to medication, which was covered in chapter 6, there are two other ways to get help for your ADD: counseling and coaching.

COUNSELING

At some point during your college career, you may find that you need a little extra help working through an issue or getting through a tough time. Most college campuses have counseling centers, although in recent years there has been an overwhelming demand for services (Schuchman 2007). If you need an appointment sooner rather than later, your college counseling center can recommend private-practice counselors in the area who are not affiliated with the university.

Here are some signs that you may benefit from counseling:

- You aren't sleeping well.

- You've been through the ending of a relationship.

- You aren't as interested in things you used to enjoy.

- You are crying or feeling weepy for no discernible reason.

- You are taking medication for anxiety and/or depression.

Even if you're already taking medication to help with anxiety or depression, counseling can provide additional relief from your symptoms. When interviewing counselors, ask them how much experience they have working with college students with ADD. Also ask them for their opinion about taking medication for ADD. Make sure that their viewpoint on medication aligns with yours. If you feel that you just don't click with a particular counselor, keep looking. You'll eventually find a good fit.

COACHING

Think of coaching as "counseling lite." The main difference between coaching and counseling is that with coaching you are working toward future goals. Coaches help you prioritize and get organized. Coaching is different from tutoring in that tutoring focuses on academic success, but coaching can help with overall functioning. A coach can help you with time management, make you accountable, and help you set deadlines; you'll need to check in with the coach to report your progress. A coach can also teach you coping skills that can be applied in all areas of your life—academics, social situations, and home life.

Coaching sessions may last an hour, but feel free to ask for a thirty-minute appointment if an hour is too long for you. Coaches can meet with you in person, over the phone, or online with instant messaging (IM); you and your coach can talk about which method of communication is best for you. If you are a visual learner, you might want to communicate via e-mail or IM. If you are an auditory learner, you may benefit from coaching over the phone or in person. You can find information on locating coaches in the Resources section.

The two most important things for me were hope and encouragement. Knowing that "the journey of a thousand miles starts with a single step" is not enough. Unless there are the skills and encouragement from a trusted friend or helper, the hope or belief that I could accomplish a task, meet a deadline, get to the goal, were all lost. The most successful people have some method and getting to the simplest method to accomplish the task is what I have always needed. I have the best coach who is willing to break it down into clear steps.

—Glenna, senior, University of Florida

In this chapter, you learned how taking care of yourself and practicing wellness can lead to a more productive and enjoyable college experience. In the next chapter, you will learn how to keep your wallet healthy.

Burning a Hole in Your Pocket: Money, College, and ADD

When you have ADD, you may feel like you have a hole in your wallet because your money disappears so quickly. It's almost as if you can hear the money in your wallet pleading, "Spend me! Spend me! Don't just let me sit here!" Excessive spending goes hand in hand with impulsivity. You may find that you're spending money and don't even realize it—$2 here, $4 there, and by the end of the week, you are out of money. People with ADD are suckers for sales, and they may also spend money to try to impress their friends.

Money management problems can arise for all people with ADD, regardless of socioeconomic background: paying bills on time may be unheard of, and balancing a checkbook may never happen. That doesn't mean that you don't try; it just doesn't come to fruition.

Having ADD can get expensive. People with ADD have a higher amount of debt, have more difficulty paying their bills, and have less money saved up than people without ADD (Barkley, Fischer, et al. 2005). They also wind up paying a lot in late fees, higher interest rates, and returned checks. And they are also more likely to pay in order to get out of boring detailed work: instead of washing your own car, you may just take it to a car wash instead, or you may also eat out because you couldn't motivate yourself to pack a lunch.

Until recently, your parents were involved in your financial support and planning in some way. Now, however, your parents are no longer as involved in your money management—it is solely up to you. When you have control over your bank account, the world can seem like your oyster—until you run out of clams. Things can get out of hand very quickly, unless you are armed with tips on how to keep your account in the black (in other words, having sufficient money to cover all your expenses).

MONEY GOALS

To keep it simple, you have three money goals while you're in college: (1) know how much you're spending, (2) don't spend more than you have, and (3) put a little away in savings. You may be thinking, "Yeah, right. I'm a college student, plus I have problems with impulsivity. I can't do those things." But you *can* do this, even if you have ADD.

DEVELOP A BUDGET AND USE IT

A budget is a tool that helps you determine how much money you can spend in different areas of your life. This may seem like a Herculean task, but just completing a budget worksheet is helpful, even if you don't follow it exactly.

Budgets include *fixed* expenses and *flexible* expenses. Fixed expenses are costs that never change. For example, if your rent is $600 a month, you can't go up to the apartment manager and tell him you only feel like paying $200 this month. (Well, you *could* do that, but it wouldn't work.) You are obligated to pay $600 a month until your lease is up, and if you don't pay that fixed expense there will be some pretty serious consequences.

Flexible expenses are costs that you can change fairly easily. For example, that $5 you spend each day on your double latte is an expense you can forgo. You don't *really* need your $5 coffee to survive, although it can certainly feel that way sometimes.

Create a Budget

Use the following worksheet to determine your monthly budget. First write down your income sources, and determine your overall monthly income—this is how much you deposit into your account each month. If this amount varies a lot from month to month, figure out how much you earn in a year and divide it by twelve to get your monthly average. Then record your monthly expenses. If you pay your car insurance every six months, divide that payment by six to get your monthly payment. Remember that this budget is just a guideline; feel free to add or delete items as you see fit. Also, your budget may differ during the summer or other times of the year, depending on your school and work schedule.

Income:

From parents _____   From work _____

From loans _____   Other income _____

Total: _____

Fixed Expenses:

Car payment _____   Health insurance _____

Rent _____   Medications _____

Cable _____   Auto fuel _____

Internet _____   School supplies _____

Electricity _____   Computer/software _____

Telephone _____   Club/org. fees _____

Tuition _____   Savings _____

Car insurance _____

Total: _____

Flexible Expenses:

Eating out _____   Groceries _____

Snacks _____   Clothing _____

Vacation/trips _____   Gifts _____

Concerts/music _____   Hobbies _____

Game tickets _____
(This may be a fixed expense
for some.)   **Total:** _____

Total Fixed and Flexible Expenses: _____

Income – Expenses = _____

Working with Your Budget

If you have money left over at the end of the month, congratulations! That is quite an accomplishment. Now, focus on putting some of that money into savings each month, even if it's just $5 or $10.

If you are left with a negative balance at the end of the month, don't worry—at least now you know, and you can do something about it. First, look at your flexible expenses—gifts, for example. Could you do a holiday gift exchange with your friends where you draw a name and only have to buy one gift? Or look at your eating habits: are you buying from vending machines or cafés on campus? To save money (and eat healthier), carry snacks from home in your backpack.

If you've adjusted your flexible expenses and you still aren't able to come out on the positive side at the end of the month, look at your fixed expenses. Do you really need the premium cable channels? Could you be paying less for car insurance? (Call your insurance company and see if they have any special discount programs available for full-time students.) Look for any possible opportunities to reduce your fixed expenses.

You may be thinking that the cost of your medication is something that you can eliminate—you may see it as a flexible expense, something you don't really need. However, for most people with ADD, medication is a fixed expense—a necessity. If you stop taking your medication or take less each day in order to stretch it out, it will not be as effective and will wind up costing you more, financially and emotionally, in the long run—due to increased speeding tickets, lower grades, and even a lower-paying job when you get out of school (Matza, Paramore, and Prasad 2005). Is it really worth saving the $100 a month? To cut medication expenses, see if you can get lower-cost prescriptions at the student health care center, or find out if the pharmaceutical company that makes your medication offers any programs in which you can receive your prescriptions at a reduced cost. See the Resources section at the end of this book for more information.

Review your budget every few months to make sure you are on track. Try using money management software. It will help you itemize and summarize your expense categories and expenditure amounts, making it much easier to see where your money is going, and how it compares to your budget. You can also see the information in a graph, which can be much easier for people with ADD to absorb and comprehend.

REDUCING EXPENSES

Sometimes people with ADD equate spending less money with depriving themselves. But it doesn't have to be that way. Look at spending less as a kind of game—you utilize strategies and you always win because you end up with more money in your account. For example, find out where your student ID can get you discounts—movie theaters, museums, the local transit authority, and other organizations usually offer reduced rates for students. Or, if you go out to a restaurant with your friends, order an appetizer instead of an entrée, and get water instead of soda. The intention is to cut some expenses—not deprive yourself. Find lower-cost ways of having the things you enjoy. If you deprive yourself entirely, you'll most likely have a spending binge later. Remember, there is a difference between wants and needs. You need to buy groceries, but buying the latest MP3 player is a want (no matter how you try to justify it as a need).

Use Caution When Treating Your Friends

Your college may offer a meal plan in which you or your parents deposit money into an account that is accessible via your student ID card. You can then use your ID card (or other assigned card) to charge your meals at cafés and dining rooms on campus. You may be tempted to treat your friends to lunch or dinner with your card, especially if you are impulsive or want to impress someone. Remember that the money on that card is the same thing as cash—you can go through it quickly if you're not careful, and then you'll be back in the position of having to ask your parents for funds. It's best to hold off on asking your parents for money, since the more you ask, the less likely they'll be to give it to you.

Try Bartering

Bartering means that you exchange services or goods with someone else. If you're in need of a service such as tutoring, consider bartering. Let's say you need help with calculus. You ask a friend for help, and in return you offer to tutor them in history. Of course, you don't always have to exchange like services. For example, if you need help getting your bike fixed, you could ask a bike-mechanic friend to make the repairs, offering your tutoring services in exchange. The concept of bartering is similar to social reciprocity, which is covered in chapter 9.

Find Free or Low-Cost Activities

One of the great things about being a college student is that you can find many free or cheap things to do on campus. Most campuses have a student union that hosts low- to no-cost activities, and many organizations in college towns offer activities at reduced rates for students. Your student ID is your ticket to fun. Look for upcoming activities on your college's website or in your student newspaper.

Make a List of Fun, Free Things to Do

Get out a piece of paper and a pen, and write down twenty fun things you can do on campus or in town for free. Get as creative as possible, but make sure you keep your activities in the legal range. Deciding to TP the student union may be free, but it's not legal. Acceptable examples may include attending an art show, riding on a bike trail, or going dancing.

Take Care of Your Possessions

Spending less money can boil down to making some simple changes in behavior. But those changes may not be so simple for people with ADD. It can be particularly difficult for the ADD person to take care of (and keep track of) their possessions, and when these things get lost, damaged, or stolen it can be pricey to replace them.

For example, do not let your laptop computer out of your sight. Leaving it in the library while you run to get a soda is the same thing as leaving a pile of money on the table. If you are wearing dressy, expensive clothes, change out of them when you get home, hang them up, and put on casual clothes. Cooking spaghetti sauce while wearing your dressy outfit is a recipe for disaster, especially if you have ADD and are not very coordinated. When you are washing your clothes in a residence hall or coin-operated laundry, follow the directions on the clothing labels and machines (so the clothes last longer), and stay there the entire time, to prevent others from walking off with your favorite clothes. Bring a textbook and study while you wait.

Plan for Emergencies

People with ADD have difficulty with planning, and you may not see the need for a backup plan in case of emergency. Your end goal is to have at least two months of expenses saved up in your savings account—a cushion in case things get rough. If you end up going through a crisis, having enough money to get by for a couple of months will be one less thing for you to worry about. As you read earlier in the chapter, even putting aside $5 or $10 a month is a good start. Build your savings account deposits into your monthly budget, so you put away a little money each month automatically.

Digging Yourself Out of a Hole

Let's say you're at the point where you have so little money left over at the end of the month that you can't even afford groceries. It's time to reevaluate your money plan.

Get out a pen and paper and list five ways you can help yourself get out of the money pit. One solution might be to take a closer look at your budget, or get one started if you haven't already. You can also try finding a higher-paying job or sell some belongings you no longer need; try an Internet classified ad service such as www.craigslist.org. Selling things you don't need not only gets you some extra cash but also frees up space in your apartment or room. Or you could ask your parents if they might provide a temporary solution to your money crunch. If not, and you can't find any other way to get food on your table until you receive your next paycheck or student loan payment, you might consider checking with a local food bank or other similar service.

Write your possible money-crunch solutions below:

1. _____

_____

2. _____

_____

3. _____

_____

4. _____

_____

5. _____

_____

Remember, it can and will get better.

I'LL CHARGE THAT ... OR MAYBE I WON'T

There's a reason why credit card companies court college students—they are easy targets. In 2004, the average undergraduate had a credit card debt of $2,169. In addition, 43 percent of undergraduates had four or more credit cards (Nellie Mae 2005). Some colleges have come under fire for not only allowing credit card companies to solicit students on campus but also receiving money from the credit card companies, either as a lump sum or per each completed application (Norvilitis 2002). Why have colleges become such a focus for credit card companies? These companies expect students to not be able to pay off their balance, and all that accruing interest means increased profit for the companies issuing the credit.

People with ADD can find it rather easy to use their credit cards. It's easy to forget that you're spending real money. You just hand the cashier a plastic card; you don't actually see the money leaving your pocket. And, since people with ADD are more likely to experience depression and anxiety, they may have a tendency to engage in "retail therapy," raising their credit card bill.

In the past, financial experts recommended staying away from credit cards and using them only in emergencies. However, with the technology available today, it is difficult to avoid using cards, especially if you purchase items online. If you do get a credit card, get one with a very low limit—no more than $500. Credit card companies may offer you low "introductory" interest rates, but those interest rates can go up after a few months, or they may increase dramatically if you miss a payment. Don't fall for the nice freebies you get when you apply for a credit card. That stuffed animal can wind up costing you several hundred dollars in interest. Don't fall for the "cash back" promises either. Credit card companies offer these in order to get you to use your card more; in reality, you'll usually wind up paying more in interest than you earn back in rewards.

In addition, having too many credit cards lowers your credit score, which may affect the interest rate you receive when you apply for a loan. (A credit score is a number between 300 and 900 that is determined by your past and current credit history, including credit card payments and loan payments, any collection agency action against you, and your current debts on loans and credit cards.) The higher your credit score, the more likely you are to be approved for the loan you're applying for, and the more likely you are to receive a lower interest rate. If you have a low credit score, you may be turned down for a loan or get a high interest rate. To keep your credit score high, keep only one or two credit cards, use them as little as possible, pay off as much of the balance as you can each month, and make payments on time.

If you are so far in debt that you can't even make your minimum payments on your credit cards every month, consider contacting a credit counseling agency, such as the National Foundation for Credit Counseling (NFCC); see the Resources section at the end of this book for information. However, beware of any "credit counselors" or agencies who make you pay a big fee up front or offer you a repayment scenario that seems too good to be true. Bankruptcy is also an extreme option, but keep in mind that, though using a credit counseling service may or may not affect your credit score, filing for bankruptcy will certainly affect your credit—for ten years.

Use of Debit Cards

Because debit cards withdraw money automatically out of your account, you have to keep track of how much you're spending. Banks make a lot of money from overdraft fees, and those fees come directly out of your bank balance. These fees, deducted from your account, can quickly compound into a major cash flow problem, so watch your account carefully, especially when your balance may be getting low. You might want to consider getting a prepaid debit card. It's much easier to keep track of the money spent, and when you run out it won't result in lots of overdraft fees.

Never use your debit card to order something online. Your account number can be compromised by identity thieves and your checking account can be wiped out. Using a credit card is a wiser choice, because if you notice unauthorized charges on your account you can dispute them with your credit card company. With debit cards, on the other hand, the money is already gone by the time you file a complaint.

Photocopy or Scan the Cards in Your Wallet

If you are prone to losing things, make sure you photocopy or scan the front and back of every card in your wallet. If your wallet is lost or stolen, you can just look at the copies to get the number to call to report your credit card as stolen or missing. Don't hesitate to call, especially if you think you may have left your wallet or purse somewhere. The credit card company can block the use of your credit cards so no one can use them; however, keep in mind that they will likely need to reissue new ones, so you'll be without your credit cards for a few days until the new ones arrive.

FINDING A BANK

Since people with ADD usually pay more bank fees than other people, and you don't have a lot of extra money to spare while you're in college, consider having your accounts at a credit union. Credit unions generally charge lower bank fees, and they allow lower balances in your accounts.

> *Make sure you have a savings or checking account with a bank that has branches and ATMs near campus and near your home. If you take a tour of your school before you enroll, take note of which banks have ATMs on or near campus. Also, make sure your parents can deposit money into your account, because if you're anything like me, you'll blow through all your money before the first semester is over.*
>
> —Mike, senior, DePaul University

Make Your Computer Work for You

Using money management software, like Quicken, is the easiest way to keep track of your bank accounts. (No, forgetting about it is *not* easier.) Ask a friend who is good at money management if he or she can help you set up your money management software and even check in on you every few weeks to make sure you're keeping it up. Almost all banks have online banking capabilities so you can sync your money management software with your accounts on an automatic schedule.

Get Overdraft Protection

As mentioned earlier, people with ADD are more likely to pay bank fees due to having a low balance in their account or being overdrawn (in other words, writing checks when you don't have enough money in your account). Open an account at a bank that offers overdraft protection for a minimal fee or no fee. This way, if you accidentally write a check or use your debit card when you don't have enough money in your checking account, the bank will automatically transfer that money over from your savings account (provided you have enough money in it). You may still pay a penalty fee, but the fees you'd pay to your grocery store for that returned check can be quadruple what you would pay for an overdraft transfer. In addition, you'll save yourself the embarrassment of bouncing a check.

Remembering Your PIN

It seems as if we need more and more personal identification numbers (PINs) and passwords with each passing day. If you have difficulty remembering stuff, it can be really tough to recall a combination of four numbers. You may be tempted to use your birthday as your PIN, in an effort to make it easier to remember, but this is not wise. Instead, consider using websites that will store your PINs and passwords; with these you would just need one password to have access to the account and all of your passwords. Information on these sites can be found in the Resources section at the end of the book.

Direct Deposit and Automatic Withdrawal

If you have ADD, you may be prone to misplacing your paycheck or forgetting to deposit it. Or you may cash it and spend all the money. Direct deposit solves both of these problems. There's no paper check to deal with, and you aren't able to cash your check—it's deposited directly into your account. You can also tell the bank to put a percentage of your check automatically into your savings account each month.

You can get your account linked with your parents' account so they can electronically transfer money to you. It's much more efficient than depositing a paper check. You may also receive financial aid payments from your college through electronic transfer.

Try using an automatic bill-paying service. The trick is that you have to make sure you have enough money in your account when the withdrawal is scheduled to occur. In cases where you split a bill with your roommates, you may want to pay your portion using a paper check.

I have direct deposit for my work paycheck. It saves me a visit to the bank—I don't need to stand in line.

—Bill, freshman, St. Petersburg College

TO WORK OR NOT TO WORK

Approximately 70 to 80 percent of undergraduates hold down jobs, and working fifteen hours or less per week has a positive effect on degree completion (American Council on Education 2006). But remember that your primary job while you're in college is just that—to be in college. Since you probably will have to work harder at your studies if you have ADD, you may want to hold off on getting a job. If you *must* get a job, wait until after your freshman year so you can get adjusted to college and know how much time you will need to devote to your studies. College is expensive, but the more time and energy you put into your schoolwork, the more you will get out of it. And your good grades may lead to a higher-paying job when you get out of school.

Real-Life Experience

If you do get a job, find one that's relevant to your future career. For example, if you're majoring in accounting, try to get a job in a business office. If you're majoring in journalism, see if you can get work at the local newspaper. A job in your career field is a more efficient use of your time. You won't be working just to earn money—you'll be working toward your future. It doesn't matter that your college job isn't exactly the job you want to have when you get out of school. The important thing is that you are getting started on the right path by acquiring valuable information that will help you to eventually get hired for your dream job. Interviewers will take notice if you have already been working in the field. In addition, you can meet people at your college job, learn valuable real-life skills, and learn more about what you like and don't like to do.

I worked for an accountant the summer after my freshman year.
That's when I realized I didn't want to be a business major.
—Henry, sophomore, University of Pennsylvania

One of the positive aspects of jobs for people with ADD is that they provide structure for your day. You may find that you function better when you know you only have two hours to study before going to work than you would if you had the whole day to study. However, you'll need to be careful not to overschedule yourself—leave yourself with enough time to complete your academic work.

Do You Really Need a Job?

Ask yourself the following questions to determine whether you need to get a job while you're in college:

- Can you cut your expenses instead of having to earn more money?

- Can you get the extra money through loans instead?

- Do you have reliable transportation?

- Can you guarantee your grades will remain either As or Bs while you're working?

- Will you be able to prioritize your time?

- What schedule adjustments will you make?

- Will you still be able to get enough sleep at night?

To find out if taking on a job will really be cost effective, write down the following information about your current situation on a separate sheet of paper:

Estimated expenses per month: _____

Estimated money available from all sources: _____

Hours per week of classes: _____

Hours per week for studying: _____

Hours per week for socializing: _____

Hours available weekly for work: _____

Estimated income from working (per week, after taxes): _____

Other ways to get money:

    Loans (where from/how much): _____

    Financial aid (where from/how much): _____

    Other (what/where/how much): _____

Income minus expenses (with job): _____

Income minus expenses (without job): _____

Will your income with a job increase enough that it justifies the time commitment?

Finding a Job in Your Field

So let's say you've looked at the situation carefully and you've discovered that, yes, you do really need to get a job. As you read earlier in the chapter, you'll want to find a job that is similar to your field of study. In the exercise below, you will brainstorm about what jobs might be best suited for you.

If you are a preveterinary major, you may want to apply for jobs that involve working with animals—see if there's an opening in the animal science department at your college, or maybe even look for a position at your local zoo. If you're an English major, you might want to consider working at the campus writing center, library, or the campus bookstore. You can consult the career resource center at your college for information on jobs related to your major. If you aren't sure about your major, are unable to find a job in your major, or need money quickly, you can always take a job that is unrelated to your major and then volunteer in an area of interest to you.

What Job Could You Do?

Now it's your turn. Write your major and come up with five jobs related to that subject. Think of jobs that match your skill level and the area in which you live. A job working with tropical plants may be hard to find if you go to college in Antarctica.

Major: _____

Jobs that are related to your field:

1. _____

2. _____

3. _____

4. _____

5. _____

ASKING THE PARENTAL UNITS FOR HELP

When you're having financial problems, you may want to ask your parents for money. However, not everyone has this option. Some families cannot afford to give extra, and some people have strained relationships with their parents and can't ask them for help. Many students prefer to do things totally on their own and don't want to ask someone for help.

If asking your parents for money is an option, you'll want to do so sparingly. Remember that your parents don't have to give you money—

they are not obligated in any way, shape, or form. So if they do give you money, show them lots of gratitude, and let them know how you'll be more cautious about money management in the future. If you've started using money management software or have cut back on your expenses, tell them.

If asking your parents for money is not a possibility, you may be tempted to ask your friends for money. This is usually not a good idea. Disputes over loaned money can destroy friendships—don't do it.

Now that you've learned how to be a financial pro while you're at college, let's look at how to make friends and get along with others while you're there.

"What Did I Do This Time?" Social Skills and ADD

College is an extremely social environment. You are around people all the time—in class, at your apartment or residence hall, in study groups, and around campus. Your social skills need to be sharp or you may miss out on a big part of the college experience.

Some people with ADD make friends easily and are able to keep those friends and have good relationships with them. But for others, social skills can be quite a challenge. People with ADD have significantly fewer close friends and report having more difficulty maintaining relationships than people without ADD do (Barkley, Fischer, et al. 2005). In this chapter, you will learn the fine art of social interaction and how to get the most out of your social life while you're in college.

SHARPENING YOUR SOCIAL SKILLS

The best way to learn social skills is to practice, practice, practice. Find a friend who has good social skills, and role-play with that person—this is a way to act out situations before they happen in real life.

How do you know if someone has good social skills? Look for someone who seems at ease talking to others, genuinely likes people of all types, is understanding, and can provide you with feedback. A socially adept person matches the following description:

- Listens more than he talks

- Waits for the other person to finish before responding

- Is able to step away from troublesome situations or people

- Is able to tell someone about a problematic behavior in a kind, fair way

- Has an even tone of voice

- Is able to judge the appropriate level of enthusiasm in the group

- Is able to remember names of familiar people

- Politely admits to the other person when he can't remember the person's name

Role-Play

Act out the following scenarios with someone with good social skills (stay in character, even if you feel awkward!):

- Asking someone out on a date

- Introducing yourself at a party

- Letting someone know he is talking too loud

- Asking a salesperson for help

- Returning something to the store

- Making small talk with someone while you're standing in line

After you role-play these situations, have your friend critique you. Then switch roles and see how the "expert" would do it. Once you've read this chapter, return to this exercise, repeat it, and see if you now have a new perspective on how to use social skills and be assertive.

I have a friend analyze my social mistakes when we talk. He tells me his reactions. I wasn't aware of how people responded to me.
— Ji, graduate student, Peking University (China)

ADD Social Skills (or Lack Thereof)

You may feel like you just weren't in line when the social skills manuals were handed out. Take the following quiz to determine whether you are a social butterfly or a social slug. Do you do any of the following?

- Keep talking even after people's eyes have glazed over?

- Interrupt more often than your friends?

- Stand too close to people?

- Have difficulty expressing your thoughts, including stumbling over your words?

- Blurt out answers to questions before the question is finished?

- Get easily frustrated with people, especially when you feel they're not making their point quick enough?

- Have a short fuse or temper with people?

- Have trouble remembering people's names?

- Talk louder than others?

- Get "carried away," rowdy, or boisterous in social situations?

If you answered yes to most of these questions, then you may be experiencing some social consequences of your ADD. To improve your social skills, try the advice in the pages that follow.

Talking and Listening

When you have ADD, you may engage in more talking than listening. Your friends' eyes may glaze over while you're talking because you've taken so long to get to your point. It can be helpful to set up a nonverbal signal with one of your friends that cues you to wrap up what you're saying. For example, you can have your friend cough or scratch her head to let you know you need to quit while you're ahead.

By practicing active listening and reducing your tendency to interrupt, you can help your conversations be much smoother and more enjoyable for you and your friends. Keep reading for tips on being not just a social butterfly but an astute social butterfly.

You need to be able to watch people's reactions to be able to figure out what is acceptable or not.

—Gwen, freshman, Bishop's University (Canada)

ACTIVE LISTENING

Make eye contact with your conversation partner (but not too sustained—that can be creepy). Pay attention to your body language. Maintain an open posture: keep your arms and legs uncrossed, sit up straight, and lean in a little when someone is telling you something important. When you are listening to someone talk, occasionally repeat back to them in your own words what they've said. This is called *paraphrasing*. Paraphrasing helps you focus, since you've given yourself a job to do. Similarly, if someone gives you directions or instructions, write them down and repeat them back to the person to make sure you've understood correctly.

LEARNING TO NOT INTERRUPT

Many times you may feel like you have to say something *right now* or it will leave your brain forever. So you interrupt and don't realize you've done it until after the words have left your mouth. When you realize you've interrupted, the thing to do is own up to it and simply say, "I'm sorry. I cut you off." Sometimes just acknowledging your faux pas can smooth out any misunderstandings.

One of the nice things about taking medication for ADD is that the medication gives you the ability to pause for a split second and keep yourself from interrupting. Medication also helps you keep your thoughts in your head until you are ready to speak.

TMI SYNDROME

One of the side effects of ADD is the tendency to disclose too much information ("TMI" in Internet speak) too soon. The first time you meet someone, you probably don't want to go into detail about the death of your pet iguana, or your difficulties with dandruff. Topics such as your health issues, difficulties in school, and family problems are usually not what you should talk about the first time you meet someone.

Safe topics include sports teams (unless you're talking about the Yankees with a Red Sox fan), the weather, your professors, and the like.

Try to stick to neutral topics until you've gotten to know the person a little better.

ASSERTIVENESS

As a child, you may have been criticized for your impulsivity or disorganization. You may have felt that you were not as "good" or as smart as the other kids. If you were constantly criticized in school for getting out of your seat, chatting with your classmates, and not listening, you can feel kind of beaten down. Many people with ADD feel this way. However, it is important to remember you have the same rights as everyone else, and it's to your benefit to be assertive in many situations.

What's Your Communication Style?

For each of the following situations, choose the answer that best describes your likely reaction.

1. It's Friday afternoon, and you've been looking forward to a relaxing weekend. A friend of yours calls and asks if you can help him move into a new apartment tonight. You respond:

   a. "Sure, I'll help," but then you quietly boil with anger the entire time you are helping your friend.

   b. "Tonight I'm taking it easy, but I can come over tomorrow at noon."

   c. "What? Are you ******* kidding me? No way."

2. You've been standing in line for season tickets for the college football team. Someone cuts right in front of you. You respond:

   a. By letting her cut in line. But you're angry about it and complain afterwards to your friends.

   b. "We've been waiting for a couple of hours. I'm not letting you cut in front of me."

   c. "Get the **** out of here!"

3. During class, the professor makes a rude comment about you showing up late to class. You respond:

   a. By saying nothing. You don't want to upset your professor any further.

   b. By meeting with the professor after class and tell him, "I apologize for being late, but your comment in class was upsetting to me."

   c. By yelling out in class, "Well, I'd be on time if your class weren't so boring!"

4. You are getting tutoring for your chemistry class. You feel that your tutor is focusing on the wrong material. You respond:

   a. By zoning out and waiting for the tutoring session to be over.

   b. By telling your tutor that you'd like to cover the other material instead.

   c. By getting frustrated and snapping at your tutor.

5. You are in traffic when someone behind you starts laying on their horn. You respond:

   a. By just sitting there and sinking into your seat so no one sees that it is you he is honking at.

   b. By trying to switch to a different lane, but not worrying about it if you can't. You're in traffic—what does the guy expect you to do?

   c. By extending your arm out the window and showing him a symbolic gesture of your unhappiness.

If your answers were mostly *a*'s, you have a passive communication style. People with ADD can be prone to doing things they don't want to do because they don't want to disappoint others. If you communicate in a passive style, you forgo what you need in order to satisfy the needs of others. However, this can leave you with feelings of resentment. You may lash out in a quiet or sneaky way—called passive-aggressive behavior—instead. For example, if you are angry with your friend about something, you may "forget" to call her back instead of just talking with her about the issue. To break the passive pattern, stand up for yourself. If someone is upset with you because you can't help with something, it's that person's problem, not yours. By asserting yourself, you will like yourself more and have healthier relationships.

If your answers were mostly *b*'s, you have an assertive communication style. You tell others what you need while still showing them respect. You may not agree with someone, but you refrain from making personal attacks. If people get upset when you politely tell them no, you figure that is their issue, and you don't beat yourself up about it.

If your answers were mostly *c*'s, you have an aggressive communication style. You have a tendency to get riled up about things. This is more common among people with ADD, because impulsivity can cause anger to spike up very quickly. You may feel slighted and think that others do things on purpose to irritate you. You need to be careful, because you never know how someone is going to react when they are the target of your aggression. Try to remember that the way people behave is not a personal attack on you. In the following sections, you will learn healthier and more effective methods of communicating.

Know Your Rights

People with ADD often forget that they have as much right to respectful treatment from others as anyone else. Have you ever thought about your inherent rights as a human being? This list may surprise you:

- The right to express your needs and wants

- The right to tell someone how his behavior affects you

- The right to change your mind

- The right to make mistakes

- The right to make your own choices

- The right to do less than is humanly possible

■ The right to feel safe, both emotionally and physically

If you feel that your right to feel safe and accepted has been compromised, possibly through emotional or physical abuse, seek the help of a counselor.

Use the "I Feel" Statement

While you are in college, you will encounter situations in which someone's behavior bothers you. In this exercise, you'll learn about the "I feel" statement. This is a handy way to let someone know that you are upset, why you are upset, and what your solution to the issue at hand might be. Here's the formula:

"When you _____,
(engage in the problematic behavior)

I feel _____
(feeling word)

because _____.
(impact of behavior on you)

I would like _____."
(solution to issue)

For example, let's say that your roommate has been wearing a live ferret as a hat. You're concerned about this because your apartment complex doesn't allow animals, you are allergic to ferrets, you feel bad for the ferret, and you find the behavior just plain weird. You decide that it's important to tell your roommate about your concerns because his behavior is having an impact on your health, your morals, and possibly your pocketbook, since the apartment management might fine you for having an animal in your apartment. An appropriate "I feel" statement might be:

"When you wear a live ferret like a hat in our apartment, I feel upset because my health is affected, it's not good for the ferret, and we might get fined by the landlord. I would like to restrict ferret-hat wearing to places that are away from the apartment."

Try to find a solution that benefits everyone, otherwise known as a win-win situation. Although using an "I feel" statement does not guarantee that a person will see things your way, at least you know you stated your position clearly and you made a valid attempt at making the situation better.

Changing the Way You Interact with People

When you start using your new assertiveness skills, you may find that you are changing the dynamics of your relationships. Sometimes people will come around easily and adapt to this new way of interaction, and even form closer relationships with you. Others may find that they are no longer able to get you to do things for them, so they distance themselves from you. This can hurt, but you'll eventually be happier that you are now taking better care of yourself and your needs and developing more fulfilling relationships.

Peer Pressure

You may have heard about or experienced peer pressure in high school. Guess what—it doesn't go away once you get to college. But what you may not know is that there is positive peer pressure as well as negative peer pressure. An example of a positive peer pressure situation is one where you tag along when your friends go to the library to study. Negative peer pressure happens when you go along with your friends to engage in a behavior that you know isn't a good idea or that you otherwise wouldn't engage in—like going out and getting drunk. People with ADD can be especially susceptible to peer pressure due to low self-esteem, lack of social skills, feelings of isolation, and not trusting themselves. The desire to feel accepted is a powerful thing. The key is to feel accepted by people who are positive influences on you.

Are you susceptible to negative peer pressure? To find out, ask yourself the following questions. When you are with your friends, do you do any of the following?

- Look to them to make decisions for you

- Engage in behaviors that you intuitively feel conflicted about or that feel wrong

- Have regret afterwards

- Engage in alcohol and/or drug use, even if you didn't initially plan to

- Engage in risky behavior

- Feel that you're a different person when you're with certain friends, and you don't like it

Tap into positive peer pressure by associating with people who might help you study more or pick up better habits—people who are generally positive influences. These people are usually optimistic, fun to be around, accept the fact that you have ADD, gently let you know if they have advice or are concerned about you, and have good boundaries—they know how to take care of themselves. The more you're around people who are positive influences, the more you will benefit both academically and socially.

Your intuition is a gut feeling or hunch you get about a person or situation. As a person with ADD, you may have been told throughout your life that you were not as good as other people, or that there was something wrong with you. This can lead you to distrust your intuition or your opinion. It is very important to remember that your intuition is just as accurate and valuable as anyone else's. Trust it and use it. If you have a feeling that a situation is just not safe, leave immediately and seek a more positive situation.

SOCIAL RECIPROCITY

"I'll scratch your back if you scratch mine." Relationships are based on give and take. A healthy relationship has an equal balance between the two. You may find that you are in relationships where you are giving and giving, but when you want to ask for something your friends aren't around. People with ADD can have difficulty knowing when they owe favors to friends or when someone is taking advantage of them. In order to remain aware of the real situation, you may want to write down favors given and favors owed to each friend. Make sure the columns remain roughly equal. Keep in mind that reciprocity naturally ebbs and flows and takes time to develop, so don't expect things to be absolutely even all the time—for example, if your friend lets you borrow her bike, you don't have to return the favor the next day. Just keep in mind that it's your turn to reciprocate, and look for an opportunity to do so in the near future.

Social Reciprocity Worksheet

To keep your relationships "even," you can keep track of who owes what. In the left column is something your friend helps you with. In the right column is a way you can reciprocate the gesture. Usually you want to reciprocate with an activity or gift that has equal value to the activity or gift your friend bestowed on you. Below is a sample worksheet for keeping track of favors:

■ Friend helps you move	■ You treat him to dinner
■ Friend visits, brings you alligator	■ You visit, you bring him porcupine
■ Friend tutors you in basket weaving	■ You tutor friend in turtle racing

Now, as you spend time with a friend over the next few days or weeks, jot down favors that you both do for each other. Make sure that the columns are equal on both sides. If they're not, you may want to consider what needs to be changed in your relationship.

- _____
- _____
- _____

- _____
- _____
- _____

HONESTY

People with ADD can be very good at "creative storytelling" when they need to find a quick way out of trouble (otherwise referred to as "exaggerating" or "lying"). They can make up stories more frequently and more elaborately than can people who don't have ADD. Although this may have saved you from some hairy situations when you were in high school, the consequences of being "creative" when you're in college can be much greater. You don't want to get "creative" if it means that you'll be called in to testify in front of your college's disciplinary board. In addition, people usually catch on and know your tales aren't truthful, and it can result in a lack of trust—people will be less likely to believe you the next time.

If you have made a serious error in judgment, own up to it. You have more to lose by trying to cover your tracks than you would if you just stated the error from the outset. The saying "What a tangled web we weave when first we practice to deceive" is true, especially for those with ADD. If you can't even remember to take your books to school, how are you going to keep that web of deceit from unraveling? It takes a lot of work (and it takes up too much brain space).

Are You a "Creative Storyteller"?

You may have used "creative storytelling" to explain your errors in judgment. However, sometimes you may find yourself being "creative" when it is not truly necessary. People with ADD have great imaginations, but sometimes they can take this too far. Check the boxes below that apply to you, to see if your storytelling is out of control:

☐ I find myself making up stories even when I'm not in trouble.

☐ I find that people like me better when I make up stories about myself.

☐ I'm having difficulty remembering what is real and what I've made up.

☐ I like the attention I get from people when I make up a story.

☐ I feel guilty after I've made up a story.

☐ I feel like I'm deceiving people.

☐ I lie and I'm not even aware of it at the time.

☐ People have caught me in my inconsistencies and lies.

☐ I'm suffering relationship/financial/academic difficulties because of my lying.

☐ I've stayed awake nights trying to figure out how to get out of a lie or how to keep it up.

If you found at least a couple of these sentences to be true of your behavior, you may have an issue with not being honest with others and yourself. Remember, you are okay as you are, and everyone makes mistakes. You don't need to embellish. What you may have used as a coping mechanism earlier in your life is probably not needed at this stage. Work to become more aware of the feeling you get when you start telling another story. Channel that creativity in a healthier way, such as by writing or painting.

ADD AND RELATIONSHIPS

You may have noticed that your relationships tend to be shorter than those of your non-ADD friends. ADD relationships tend to start off intensely and then die down quickly. People with ADD become bored after the initial rush of the new relationship has worn off. And, because people with ADD may feel dependent on their partner, they may cheat instead of breaking off the relationship.

Now that you're in college, you have more opportunities for intense but quick relationships than you had in high school. You have more unsupervised time, you make your own rules, you have exposure to alcohol and drugs, and you are around a ton of people your age (who are also under the influence of hormones). (See chapter 7 for information on safe sex and preventing pregnancy.) Not all relationships can or should last forever, but when they burn out it can be painful and upsetting. Let's look a little closer at breakups and how they can affect you.

Breakups

People with ADD can have difficulties with transitions and change, so breakups can hit them particularly hard. It can hurt even more when you feel that your girlfriend or boyfriend broke up with you because of your ADD. Sometimes partners without ADD become like our external brain. You may have relied on your girlfriend or boyfriend to help with tasks that were difficult for you, making a breakup with that person even more difficult to take.

Quite a few relationships that started in high school reach breakup status when one or both of the partners go away to college. Maintaining a long-distance relationship can be difficult—it's time consuming, and people change when they are living on their own. In addition, people with ADD are impulsive and prone to "out of sight, out of mind" behavior if their significant other is far away. Although some people are able to maintain long-distance relationships, these can be too complicated for the person with ADD.

Going through a breakup is a grieving process. Anyone dealing with a breakup can experience shock, denial, anger, depression, and finally acceptance, at different times. People with ADD may feel these emotions with more intensity but for a shorter duration.

If you feel that you're having a more difficult time than your friends have had when they've endured breakups, seek counseling. Make sure the counselor has experience working with ADD.

WHEN YOU ARE THE PERSON INITIATING THE BREAKUP

You may find that a relationship is not working for you. Signs of trouble may include constant arguing, feeling like you can't be yourself around the person, or experiencing any kind of abusive treatment in the relationship. There are right ways and wrong ways to break up with someone. Here's how to do it right:

First, meet the person in a neutral location. It really isn't fair to break up with someone at your apartment. It puts the other person in an awkward situation. Then state specifically that things are not working out. Do not make any comments such as "Maybe in the future we can get together." If you're going to break it off, make it a clean break. The other person may ask you if this is what you really want. Stick to your decision. Repeat that it would be best if the two of you stopped seeing each other. It's possible that the other person may start crying or even yelling. It might be helpful to simply say, "I'm sorry." If things get out of hand, walk away. Later, if you see your former partner around campus or at a social gathering, be polite, and refrain from "ex sex." Physical intimacy with a former partner rarely leads to a healed relationship and only makes things more complicated.

Maintaining Relationships

One way to figure out how to improve your relationships is to take a look back. Get out a pad of paper and a pen. First, write down the name of your partner in your last significant relationship, either romantic or platonic. Next, write how long the relationship lasted. Then write the reasons why the relationship ended. Did the relationship end because of your ADD symptoms or because your partner had unrealistic expectations? Did the relationship end because it started too quickly?

Then write your feelings about the ending of that relationship—how did it affect you? Finally, rewrite history. Turn the reason the relationship ended into something more positive. What did you learn from the relationship? What would you do differently next time? How can you improve on this pattern the next time you meet someone?

For example, let's look at what a certain green amphibian wrote:

Last significant relationship: Miss Piggy

Relationship lasted: Too long

Why did it end? I ate a ham sandwich in front of her. How was I supposed to know that was offensive?

Rewrite history: We did have some good times. It was my first cross-species relationship, and I learned a lot about pigs.

Another example:

Last significant relationship: Sally

Relationship lasted: 6 months

Why did it end? We broke up because she said she got tired of me being late for everything. I feel bad about this, because if I didn't have ADD she might still be my girlfriend.

Rewrite history: There's no guarantee that the relationship would have worked out, even if I didn't have ADD. I did learn valuable things from the relationship, like the fact that being on time may be more important to others than it is to me.

Are You in an Abusive Relationship?

If you have ADD and feel that you can do nothing right and that your life is a series of mistakes and underachievements, it can be easy to get drawn into an abusive relationship. You may also be vulnerable to abusive relationships because you're away from your family and friends while you're in college and are more likely to become dependent on someone else for support.

Abusive relationships usually start off very intensely, as is the case with many relationships of people with ADD. However, the abusive relationship involves a person needing control over someone else. According to the stereotype, men are the abusers, but women can also be abusive. Ask yourself if the following has ever occurred in your relationship:

- Your partner teases you, even after you've asked him or her to stop.

- Your partner holds you down and forcefully tickles you, even after you've asked him or her to stop. He or she claims it was "just a game."

- Your partner tries to limit your contact with your family and friends. He or she comes up with reasons why you shouldn't hang around certain people.

- Your partner or both of you engage in alcohol or drug abuse. (This can escalate the incidence of domestic violence.)

- Your partner has pushed you, hit you, slapped you, or engaged in any other type of physical violence.

- Your partner routinely uses guilt to manipulate you.

- Your partner calls you derogatory names.

- Your partner tells you that you deserve the negative treatment you're getting.

- Your partner is unfaithful, makes no attempts to hide this behavior, and/or blames it on you.

- Your partner tells you what you should wear and how you should behave.

- Your partner forces himself or herself on you during sex or coerces you during sex.

■ Your friends and family have expressed concern about your partner's behavior, saying that you just aren't the same since you've been with your partner and/or saying that they don't want to be around your partner because of his or her behavior.

If you see even one of these behaviors in your partner, you may be in an abusive relationship. Although some abusive partners can (and do) get better with help, it may be in your best interest to leave instead of sticking around to see if anything changes. If you have been threatened and are afraid to leave for fear of further harm being done to you, contact the police and find a safe location to stay, such as a friend's house. You can find the contact information for your local abuse shelter in the community pages at the front of most phone books.

OVERSTIMULATION

People with ADD have a threshold for noise and commotion that is lower than that of other people. Repetitive noises can quickly irritate you. You may notice sounds that non-ADD people don't—like the humming noise made by fluorescent lights in a classroom. Not surprisingly, you may notice that you become frustrated more easily due to the sheer amount of people and commotion in college. It's important for you to notice when you're starting to feel overstimulated in a social situation, and to know when you need to take a break.

When Do You Need to Take a Break?

How do you recognize when you've been overstimulated? It's time to get a little peace and quiet when people's voices seem to be running together, like you are faced with a giant wall of noise, or you have a hard time tuning out a repetitive noise. In addition, your heart may race, you may feel a headache coming on, and you may suddenly feel irritable enough to snap at someone.

If you are experiencing any of these symptoms, step outside for a break. If you're taking a break at night, don't go outside alone—take a trusted friend who will quietly walk with you while you rest your brain.

SOCIAL ANXIETY

Many people with ADD also feel shyness, even extreme shyness, known as social anxiety or social phobia. You may feel shy because in the past people may have made comments about your not knowing the "right" way to behave. The nice thing about college is that it gives you an opportunity to reinvent yourself. The reputation you had in high school doesn't matter once you get to college. No one really cares what you were like before. So now is your chance to start fresh.

Do You Have Social Anxiety?

Check the boxes next to the experiences that apply to you:

☐ Excessive worrying days or weeks before a social event

☐ Fear that people are thinking negative things about you

☐ Replaying a conversation in your head and worrying about what you said

☐ Avoiding social activities

☐ Fear of social situations that is affecting how you live your life

☐ Physical symptoms of anxiety in anticipation of or during social situations, such as a pounding heart, sweating, or stomach upset

Do you experience anxiety in any of the situations below? After each line, write whether this situation causes you no distress, mild distress, moderate distress, or severe distress. For the purposes of this exercise, "distress" is defined as any unpleasant feelings you might experience.

Eating in public _____

Talking on the phone in public _____

Writing a check or other document with others watching _____

Speaking or asking a question in front of your class _____

Asking someone out on a date _____

Using a public restroom _____

Returning something to a store _____

Asking someone for help with a project _____

If you marked three or more situations with "mild distress," two or more with "moderate distress," or any with "severe distress," you may have social anxiety. Read on for a discussion of available treatments.

Help for Social Anxiety

Fortunately, there are treatments available for social anxiety. And most, if not all, of these treatments can be used in addition to your ADD medication. Cognitive behavioral therapy has been found to be effective for treating social anxiety (McEvoy 2007). Cognitive behavioral therapy uses techniques such as becoming more aware of irrational thinking patterns, and "reframing," or turning a negative statement into a positive. Other treatments for social anxiety include medication and engaging in role-plays of social situations. If you are burdened by anxiety about social activities and situations, you are strongly encouraged to seek help.

DRUG AND ALCOHOL USE

In chapter 7, you read about the tendency of ADD people toward alcohol and drug addiction. Since alcohol is a depressant, it can help people with ADD feel more relaxed and social, especially if they are usually shy. Alcohol and drugs may delude them into thinking that their brain is acting "normal."

However, if you already have a problem with interrupting people, not listening, and being distracted, alcohol and drugs can make these tendencies even stronger. It can cause you to go from just distracted to downright obnoxious. Alcohol and drug abuse also increases the possibility of rape and other forms of violence because these substances lower people's inhibitions and can muddy their perceptions of right and wrong. As mentioned earlier, it's best to avoid alcohol and drugs altogether when you have ADD.

When Your Friends Don't Believe in ADD

During your college years (and beyond), you'll meet people who don't believe that ADD exists. They may make comments that you are just lazy, your medication is addictive, or you just aren't trying hard enough in school. These comments can hurt, because it seems like someone is making an unfair judgment about you. It's especially hurtful when the comments come from someone you care about.

How can you respond when a friend or professor makes comments like these? Assume that the person simply isn't educated about ADD. Arm yourself with information. Explain that ADD is biological—brain scans have identified differences in the structure and functioning in the ADD brain. If you have a close relationship with the person, you may feel comfortable explaining how your medication helps you. You can also state that studies have shown that taking medication actually decreases your chances of becoming an addict (Biederman 2003).

FORMING NETWORKS

A network is a group of people who rely on each other for support, information, companionship, or help. People can find ready-made networks by joining organizations, religious groups, or intramural sports teams, or they can form their own just by meeting people in their community. Even if you simply attend an event, you'll be likely to meet people (unless you stand in the corner facing the wall the whole night).

You've heard the saying "It's not what you know; it's who you know." This idea may cause you some anxiety, because using social skills and making friends may not be your forte, and you may worry about your ability to get a job if your network is lacking. In chapter 10, you'll learn how to use your network to get the word out that you are looking for a job.

When I arrived at college, I had a network already established at my church. I could ask any questions about college, and students in my church had the answers. It really helped my adjustment to school.

—Rusty, junior, University of Florida

Rate Your Networking Skills

Answer yes or no to the following sentences.

_____ 1. I'm a member of a club or organization.

_____ 2. I'm okay with asking for support from others.

_____ 3. I see everyone as being interconnected.

_____ 4. I feel I have a lot to give to others.

_____ 5. I have business cards listing my e-mail and website and phone numbers.

_____ 6. I have a professional-looking website that lists my contact information.

_____ 7. I gratefully acknowledge gifts and services that are given to me.

_____ 8. I say no to events or projects that drain my energy and time.

_____ 9. I return phone calls and e-mail within twenty-four hours.

_____ 10. I write a list of things I need to tell someone before I call them.

If you answered yes to six or more of these sentences, you are on your way to being a super networker. You know that forming a network leads to greater success for you and others in your network.

If you answered yes to three to five of these sentences, you are on your way to being a great networker. Look at the sentences to which you answered no. These are the areas that you can work on in order to reach your full potential as a networker.

If you answered yes to zero to two of these sentences, you may find networking a little challenging. Never fear, you'll be on your way to being a master networker soon. Do you have a friend who seems to know just about *everybody*? Ask that person how he or she does it. Chances are that this friend uses the skills listed in the exercise above.

Clubs and Organizations

You may find it easier to connect with people who have similar interests. One of the best ways to meet people at college is to join a club or organization that matches your interests. There are groups for social causes, hobbies, and various other interests. If you meet people with similar interests, you may find that they understand you better than others do, and you may feel more comfortable.

Your student union may have a student activities center that lists names of campus organizations and clubs. You may also find that information in your college newspaper or website.

Going Greek

Belonging to a fraternity or sorority is a great way to network and make lifelong friends. Fraternities and sororities can provide leadership opportunities, academic support, job connections, community service opportunities, social support, and more. You may have the chance to live in the fraternity or sorority house, which is usually situated on campus. *Rush* is the period of time in which you consider which houses you are interested in, and in which fraternities and sororities choose new members. For sororities, this period of time is usually the week before fall classes; for fraternities, rush may take place during the fall semester.

Joining a fraternity or sorority involves a financial and time commitment, as is the case with other organizations. More information on fraternities and sororities can be found in the Resources section. You can also contact your college's Greek life division for more information.

Being a member of a fraternity really was one of the highlights of my time in college. It gave you the opportunity to form some great friendships and the memories will certainly last a lifetime!! Going to college was tough because you left your home and found yourself in a dorm . . .not a great place at the best of times. The frat house became another home where you formed very strong friendships and others helped look out for you.

—J.P., senior, Stevens Institute of Technology

Social Networking Websites

Social networking websites are Internet locations where you can post your profile online, make "friends," join virtual groups, and form networks. These sites can provide an amazing opportunity to meet people, find out about campus events, and form groups online. You can also use them to easily keep in contact with your friends and family back home.

Keep in mind that anything you post on your site is permanently saved on the Internet, even after you delete it. If you practice "drunk posting" and post a long missive on your blog about how hot your lab partner is, your post can come back to haunt you, even if you delete it later. Think of the "publish" or "submit" button as a "final submission" button—once you click, you can't take it back. Do not post any photos of you doing anything illegal or unwise.

Also keep in mind that any photo taken of you is the photographer's property and can be posted online without your permission. For this reason, don't allow yourself to be in situations where someone could take a photo of you doing something unflattering or inappropriate. If you're unsure about the appropriateness of a photo, ask yourself, "Would I want my mother, my boss, or my future children looking at this?"

More and more frequently, employers are seeking information about their prospective (and current) employees on the Internet through social networking websites. So keep your behavior and your appearance tame and dignified at all times—especially when there's a camera around. You will learn more about how these sites can affect your ability to get hired in chapter 10.

10

To Infinity and Beyond: Going Out into the "Real World"

When it comes to planning for the future, people with ADD can have difficulty planning ahead. They may wait until the last possible minute before applying for jobs, and they may show up at a job interview unprepared. They may be faced with so many options and tasks that their brains go into overload and they can't make a choice.

Your undergraduate career is coming to a close, and you are ready to conquer the world with your degree in hand. But wait a second—how do you even start to put together Act II of your life? In this chapter, you'll learn how to find the right job or graduate school program for you, how to have a successful interview, and how to start your career.

POSTCOLLEGE OPTIONS

You may be at the end of your college experience, thankful that you no longer need to go back to "that place." You are so ready to move on and get a real job. However, stop for a bit and give some thought to continuing your education.

Earning an Advanced Degree

Many jobs now require an advanced degree—a master's degree or Ph.D. In addition, medical and law school, as well as other advanced education programs, are possible choices.

If you have ADD, it is easier to go straight through to graduate school right after your bachelor's degree instead of taking time off first. You're still in school mode, so it's best to keep going while your momentum is up.

You should start applying for graduate schools during your junior year. Graduate schools usually require that you take the Graduate Record Examinations (GRE); postgraduate business programs require the Graduate Management Admission Test (GMAT); medical schools require the Medical College Admission Test (MCAT); and law schools require the Law School Admission Test (LSAT). You may be able to receive accommodations for these tests. See the Resources section for more information. (And you thought you were done with those standardized tests!)

Are You Ready for Graduate School?

If you are considering continuing on to get an advanced degree, answer the following questions:

- Do you want to attend three (or more) years of college?

- Are you prepared to move away to go to the school of your choice?

- Are you willing (and able) to put the effort into writing a thesis or dissertation?

- Will attending graduate school negatively affect your financial standing?

- Do you need an advanced degree to have a career in your field?

Look back over your answers. What are your feelings about attending graduate school now? Write your thoughts and feelings in a notebook.

To Intern or Not to Intern

When you reach your junior year of college, you should start looking into summer or postcollege internships. You may want to go out and get a job immediately instead of doing an internship for little or no money. That ADD reasoning is understandable. You are probably feeling done with school and just want out, and you are ready to make some money. However, internships can provide you with valuable experience and networking opportunities. Many interns have found full-time jobs at the same company after their internship was over.

In addition, your academic department may require that you do an internship before you graduate. Some departments have an internship coordinator who can help you find the right company and position. For ideas on internships, talk to alumni from your department and visit your college's career resource center.

Taking Time Off

After you've accomplished a huge task such as graduating from college, your ADD brain may be exhausted and want to take a long vacation. It's worked hard, and it's tired. The pitfall is that sometimes people take a vacation of two weeks that turns into five years. Because ADD is a disorder of motivation, it can be difficult to get back in the swing of things after taking time off. As you've read, "A body at rest stays at rest; a body in motion stays in motion." Limit your vacation to a few weeks at most in order to keep your brain on the right track.

If you've taken out student loans, you must begin to repay them after a six-month *grace period*. That means that six months after you graduate you must start repaying your loan, or show the lender that you're continuing your education. Also keep in mind that once you graduate, your health insurance coverage—whether provided through your college or through your parents—terminates. Your choices for retaining insurance are: (1) find a job that offers health insurance, (2) continue your education and get the college's insurance, or (3) win the lottery and get your own policy.

Going Out into the Workforce

You may be ready to be done with college, and you may want to start making some money. In the following pages, we'll discuss navigating the interview process, negotiating job offers, and beginning your career. You may have difficulties with impulsivity and planning, but the information in this chapter will help you be better prepared for your journey.

FIND THE BEST JOB FOR YOU

People with ADD work best in jobs where they're able to move around and have some variety in their daily work routine. Working in a cubicle is one of the worst possible job atmospheres for people with ADD. There is no door; you're surrounded by noise and people; and you're in a small, cramped space for most of your day. However, a large proportion of jobs available to you after college involve working in a cubicle.

How can you find a job you love without having to work in a cubicle farm? The most obvious solution is to search specifically for jobs that suit your interests, strengths, weaknesses, and need for movement.

For more information on available careers, meet with a career counselor at your college's career resource center. Also, take a look at the *Occupational Outlook Handbook*, published by the U.S. Department of

Labor. The handbook gives descriptions of over 250 occupations, including information on qualifications, future outlook, working conditions, and earning potential. The handbook is available for free online; see the Resources section for information.

Military. People with ADD tend to have success in the military. Why is this? Their time is very structured, there are immediate consequences for their behavior, and the rules are very clear. However, to enlist in the United States military, you must not have taken medication for ADD in the past year. If you enter the military with a bachelor's degree, you may be commissioned as an officer. You may also qualify for student loan forgiveness.

Five Years from Now

You may not yet have a clear idea of what you want to do, careerwise. This is normal for people with ADD. So let's get those ideas flowing. Get a pad of paper and a pen. First, close your eyes and visualize your ideal workday five years into the future. See yourself as you wake up, get dressed, get your work materials together, and go to your job. When you get there, you get started for the day. Open your eyes and write down the answers to the following questions about your visualization:

- What city did you live in?

- What type of housing did you have?

- What time did you wake up in the morning?

- What did you do to get ready?

- What did you wear to work?

- What did you take with you to work?

- How did you get to work (car, bus, subway, spaceship)?

- What was your commute like? How long was it?

- Where did you work?

- What did your work surroundings look like? Were you indoors or outdoors?

- How did you start your workday? Did you have an assistant? Were you at a desk?

Keep this visualization in mind when you're searching for a career or postcollege education. Revisit it every so often to see how your image of the ideal workday has changed.

CAREER RESOURCE CENTER: KNOW IT AND USE IT

Many campuses have career resource centers, which are a gold mine of information about interviews, resumés, and potential careers. This office is usually staffed by people with special training in career counseling and career issues. Some staff members may even have earned the designation of Nationally Certified Career Counselor.

Services provided differ from campus to campus. Some centers hold individual and group counseling sessions about career issues. They can help you develop a career plan and give you career aptitude testing to help you find out what career best suits you. Some may review your resumé and help you polish it up for prospective employers, offer workshops on interview skills, and even conduct mock interviews to help you improve your performance. They may also arrange for companies to come to campus to meet students and conduct interviews for internships and jobs.

Some career resource centers even hold seminars regarding coping with ADD in the workplace. Take advantage of these services. The majority of the services (if not all of them) are usually offered at no charge. You may also be able to use the center after you graduate. See your college's career resource center for more details. Throughout this chapter, you'll read about the services your career center may be able to provide you.

USE YOUR NETWORK

In chapter 9, you learned about the importance of forming a network, a group of people you can rely on for information or support. Now that you're looking for a job, it's time to put your network into action. Tell as many people in your network as possible that you're looking for a job. Let them know your degree and your graduation date. Indirect contacts are some of the best ways to get a job. You never know whose brother's sister's friend's neighbor's dog sitter might have the perfect job for you.

Many college career resource centers can help you get in contact with alumni in your field via the Internet or through workshops or mentoring activities. If you receive someone's business card at one of these workshops or at any other gathering, write on the back of it the date and event where you met the person, and anything interesting you talked about. This trick will help jog your memory.

MENTORING

Determining whether a career is right for you is much easier when you have a mentor—someone in your field of interest who is willing to meet with you and talk about his or her experiences in that field and offer advice. You can find a mentor by asking people in your network, or by contacting your career resource center on campus. They may have a database of alumni who have volunteered to be mentors for students.

One of the best ways to learn more about a career is to "shadow" someone. This means that you spend a workday with them, learning about their daily tasks, opportunities, and challenges. (Of course, you want to ask them first instead of just showing up and latching onto them like a remora.)

Another way to get more information about a field is to conduct informational interviews with knowledgeable people working in that career area. In these interviews, you ask them questions about the challenges and positive aspects of the job. Again, the career resource center may be able to help you find alumni and other professionals willing to give informational interviews.

BEING PROFESSIONAL

In chapter 9, you learned about Internet networking sites, including appropriate and inappropriate placement of information and images. This is where that decorum really counts—when you're looking for a job.

Prospective employers view applicants' websites to see if they represent what the company is looking for. If you have a website or networking site page, remove any references to alcohol or drugs, and any photos of you or your friends in which you are wearing a minimal amount of clothing, holding up a bottle of alcohol, or displaying any questionable facial expression or posture. You might also want to consider taking down any inappropriate comments, such as "Somebody better hire me or I'm going to lose my mind!"

Get yourself a professional-sounding e-mail address that contains just your first and last name. Don't use a cutesy e-mail address like sweetcheeks@server.com, and also avoid addresses that sound even slightly racy. If an employer sees that your e-mail address has any questionable words or shows your immaturity, your resumé may go directly into the circular file (trash bin). If you have a common name such as "John Smith," you can use different variations on your name, since johnsmith@server.com is probably already taken. Try using "jsmith," "john.smith," "johnsmith," or your first and last name followed by a number. Just don't use controversial numbers such as "666."

Interviews

Interviews are your chance to show a prospective employer all of the great things you can bring to the company. You may have one interviewer or you may have two or three. Because of your ADD, you may need an extra push to feel confident during your interviews. You can get that boost of confidence by changing your mind-set: think of an interview as an opportunity for you to learn more about potential employers. However, you also want to make sure you don't come across as too confident, a pitfall you can encounter when you're feeling insecure.

YOUR RIGHTS IN THE INTERVIEW PROCESS

It is illegal for a prospective employer to ask you about any medical disabilities, your age, your marital status, or if you have children. Employers are only allowed to ask these questions if the answer directly affects your ability to do the job. For example, if you are applying for a job as a wine sommelier and you have a poor sense of smell, then that would be a problem. Employers are allowed to ask you about your ability to focus or pay attention if it's a requirement for the job. But you should not be asked specifically about ADD nor should you voluntarily disclose that you've been diagnosed with it.

If you feel that you've encountered bias or discrimination either due to an interviewer asking questions about your medical history, marital status, race, ethnicity, or gender, or due to an interviewer's inappropriate comments, remedies are available. The U.S. Equal Employment Opportunity Commission (EEOC) enforces the federal law prohibiting discrimination in the workplace. Contact information for the EEOC can be found in the Resources section.

BEFORE THE INTERVIEW

Getting prepared for an interview is crucial. You need to have your resume together, look sharp, and have brushed up on your interview skills. Don't worry—after you read about how to prepare for your interview, you'll knock 'em dead. (On second thought, just leave them stunned by your awesomeness.)

Resumés. A resumé is a one-page summary of your degrees, awards, work experience, and community involvement. In short, it's a list of your accomplishments. You will bring your resumé with you when you attend job fairs and interviews.

Resumés need to be laid out in an organized format, so they can be difficult for people with ADD to create on their own. Your campus career resource center can help you with your resumé. They may offer classes on how to write an effective resumé, and will review yours to make sure it is top-notch.

Utilize the career resource center at your school for help with your resumé. If you don't have access to a career resource center, it is worth it to pay someone to help you write your resumé. People at the career centers are up on current trends when it comes to resumés.

—Katie, senior, Westfield State College

Frequently update your resumé. To combat memory loss, as soon as you accomplish something, sit down and add it to your resumé. Keeping an updated resumé can really set you ahead of the pack. Let's say you hear about your dream job—since you have your resumé already updated, you can just print it out and send it in (with a great cover letter), and you're done.

Resumé categories. Good resumés have categories so the information is easier to read. Put the following categories on your resumé: (1) degree, (2) awards, (3) special training/certifications, (4) work experience, (5) community involvement, and (6) references (list three). Now, get to work filling out what goes in each category.

Securing a letter of recommendation. Interviewers may ask you to provide them with letters of recommendation from your professors or former supervisors. When asking people to write recommendation letters for you, give them a minimum of two weeks before the letter is due. Ask people who have had recent interactions with you—they will usually provide you with a more detailed and accurate letter. If you are applying for more than one position, provide information about all of them to the person writing your letters. This makes it much easier for that person, because he or she can send off all the letters at one time.

When e-mailing someone to ask them to write a letter of reference, write a short description of the position and attach your resumé. Fill out the letter writer's name, position, company, and contact information on any applicable forms. Send the forms along with a preaddressed stamped envelope. Include your resumé and send any paperwork that details what should be included in the recommendation letter.

Here's an example of an e-mail asking for a recommendation letter.

Dear Dr. Frankenstein:

I am applying for the position of Laboratory Assistant at Scary Labs in Bolt Neck, New York. The position would require labeling and organizing brains. Do you feel you know my work well enough to write a recommendation letter for me? I would greatly appreciate it.

The letter is due four weeks from now on October 31, 2008. If you agree, I will mail you the recommendation form, instructions, and a preaddressed stamped envelope.

Thank you,

Igor

It's okay to contact your reference after two weeks to check on the status of your recommendation letter. Always send a thank-you note, and follow up later to let them know about that great new job you snagged, with their help.

You may notice that some application forms include a signature line along with a statement that you voluntarily agree to waive your right to view your letters of recommendation. It is recommended that you sign this waiver. If you have chosen a good reference, you probably don't need to see the letter anyway. Waiving your rights gives the reference the opportunity to write a more candid letter. Not waiving your right to view the letter is like standing over your reference's shoulder as he writes. Even though there's nothing in the letter you should be concerned about, it's still annoying to your letter writer and is not in your best interests.

Questions Interviewers Ask

In a separate notebook, write down your answers to the following common interview questions. Sometimes when ADD people are nervous, they talk even more than usual, so make your answers no longer than one paragraph—this will help keep you on track.

1. What are your strengths and weaknesses?

2. Why did you leave your last job?

3. How can you help our company?

4. What makes you stand out from everyone else applying for this job?

5. How do you handle difficult people?

6. Where do you see yourself in five years?

7. What are your salary requirements?

8. Do you have any questions for me?

Next, do a mock interview with a friend who has interview experience and good social skills. Ask your friend what he or she would change about your performance. Make sure you play both roles in the interview. In addition, attend any mock-interview workshops held by the career resource center on campus.

Do your research. Before you interview with a company, go online and look at their latest annual report. This is the information the company gives out about itself, including financial statements. Also look up news about the company using an Internet search engine. You want to come to the interview armed with information. At the end of the interview, the interviewer will usually ask you if you have any questions. Use the information you have gleaned about the company to form insightful questions that show that you've done your research and are interested in the job. You may want to ask questions such as "I read in *Blah Business News* that your market share has increased by 15 percent. To what do you attribute your success?" "What qualities are you looking for in new employees?" "What are the company's plans for future growth?"

Salary is another topic you'll need to research before your interview. If you feel you are an underachiever or you have undervalued your abilities, you may give the prospective employer too low of a salary figure. Consult with other people in the field and do some research online, so that when the interviewer asks you for your salary figure, you can offer a number that is neither too high nor too low.

Brush up on your manners. Using good manners during your interview is of utmost importance. If you have ADD, you may find it difficult to retain all of the unwritten rules of etiquette in your memory. You may also notice that you make etiquette mistakes but never seem to learn from your errors. This is common in people with ADD.

Practicing Your Manners

Before you go out for an interview, brush up on your etiquette. You can take a class or learn etiquette from a manual, but hands-on learning is best. Role-play with a friend who seems to know about good manners. Have a meal with this person during which you practice where to put your napkin when you temporarily get up from the table and where to put it when you leave the restaurant; where to put your silverware between bites and when you're done with your meal; the proper way to hold an eating utensil; the proper way to cut food; how to excuse yourself from the table; how not to talk with one's mouth full; and other related points of etiquette. See the Resources section at the end of this book for more information on etiquette.

Interview Checklist

Copy this list and laminate it. You can check off the items with a dry-erase marker as you go. Wipe off the list and voilà—it's ready for your next interview.

- ☐ Business suit cleaned and pressed (have someone without ADD iron it)

- ☐ Briefcase/attaché clean and conditioned or polished

- ☐ Three copies of resumé

- ☐ Haircut

- ☐ Manicure

- ☐ Shaved/tweezed

- ☐ Only the lightest spritz of perfume or cologne, if you must use any

- ☐ Clean shoes, new laces

- ☐ Nice pen and notebook

- ☐ Business cards with your address, e-mail, and cell phone

- ☐ Printed directions to interview location; address of location; name and title of interviewer

- ☐ Practice drive to interview location done

- ☐ Car tidy and clean

DURING THE INTERVIEW

So it's your big day. Time to show them what you've got. Make sure you have yourself well organized before you walk out the door, and leave your home well before you think you need to in order to be on time. Keep in mind the traffic patterns in your area at that time of day, and make sure you leave with plenty of time to spare.

Some interviewers watch to see how together you are when you arrive at the office. If they see you getting out of the car and they get a glimpse of all the papers and wrappers that have been accumulating in your car for weeks, you don't get bonus points. Discard any garbage in the car and vacuum and wash it the day before your interview. You want to look calm, organized, and professional as you exit your car, walking confidently, with your attaché case in hand, to the office door.

Shaking hands. Be sure to shake the interviewers' hands when you meet them. Make sure your hands are clean and dry. Use a firm handshake—you don't want the interviewer to feel as if he or she is holding a limp fish or as if he or she is in a death grip. Practice your handshake with a friend.

Answering questions about underachievement, grades, or sanctions. Let's say you have less-than-stellar grades, you have had some behavioral issues while you've been at college, you changed your major more than a few times, or you have the classic pattern of "not working to your potential." How do you handle these questions during job interviews?

You need not mention attention-deficit disorder by name. You are not obligated to give any information about a diagnosis or treatment (including the use of medication, unless you are taking a stimulant medication and being given a drug test as part of the application process). However, you can address the issue by stating that yes, you did have issues in that area, but you have been and continue to take steps to improve that and make sure it doesn't happen again. If you have good grades in your chosen field of work, emphasize that to the interviewer.

What are your strengths and weaknesses? Come up with *something* to say if you are asked, "What are the areas in which you would like to improve?" Do not answer, "I don't know" or "I don't really have any weaknesses." Before the actual interview, write down some areas you would like to improve in, such as "active listening," "organization," or "interrupting." Then write down how you are working to improve this behavior or plans you have to improve this behavior. During the interview, make sure you follow up your mention of the challenging area with an explanation of how you are planning to improve it. For example, "An area I'd like to improve upon is organization. I'm currently taking a class called Organizing 101." Keep in mind that you should tailor the area of improvement you mention according to the job you're interviewing for. If you're applying to be a veterinary technician, it's not a good idea to tell the interviewer that you want to work on your intense dislike of animals. (If that's the case, that job might not be the right one for you, anyway!)

AFTER THE INTERVIEW

It may be surprising to you that the period of time after the interview can be just as crucial as the interview itself. There are a few things you can do to help leave a positive impression and determine your next steps. Let's look at those now.

Show your gratitude. Writing a thank-you note after the interview is a crucial part of the process. Not only is it good form to show gratitude, but it also lets the interviewer know that you're serious about the job. Plus, it provides you with some more visibility in the job hunting process, and it's an opportunity to remind the interviewer of your strengths and what you can bring to the company.

Send an actual letter instead of an e-mail thank-you, unless the interviewer has specifically requested that you contact him or her via e-mail. Use white or cream-colored stationery that contains your contact information—do not use your stationery with cute little whales or froggies on it. Here is a sample of a thank-you note to an interviewer.

April 8, 2008

Mr. Kermit T. Frog
Lily Pad Enterprises
123 Lily Drive
Big Lake, New York 10012

Dear Mr. Frog:

It was a pleasure meeting you yesterday. Thank you for taking the time to discuss the fly-catcher position at Lily Pad Enterprises. I enjoyed learning more about your new projects, particularly the Lily Pad XR 3000. Your staff was very green and courteous, and I appreciated their enthusiasm.

In addition to the information I shared with you at our meeting, I thought of two other credentials that show my ability to catch flies. I was named the Mid-Regional Fly Catching Champion in 2005, and I was the runner-up in 2004. I feel I have the fly-catching capabilities that you are looking for in prospective members of your team.

Thank you for taking the time to meet with me. I am very interested in your company, and I look forward to hearing from you about the fly-catcher position.

Sincerely,

Michigan J. Frog

As you can see, the first thing you do is thank the interviewer for meeting with you. Include a sentence about how you enjoyed visiting the company. Then write about your strengths and what assets you could bring to the company. Close by thanking the interviewer once again for taking the time to meet with you and consider you for the job.

Now it's your turn! Write a rough draft of your thank-you note, and have a friend (or a career counselor) review it before you send it off. Good luck!

I Think I Can, I Think I Can...

People with ADD want instant results, so you may feel discouraged or feel like quitting after a few interviews with no offers. Being sensitive to rejection is common for people with ADD.

If you don't get the job, consider contacting the interviewer to ask for feedback about your interview. This shows motivation, and the interviewer may remember you more easily if another job becomes available. If you find that you're getting turned down for jobs more often than your friends, talk with them and practice your interview skills. Were they hired because they had more experience? Did they know someone at the company? Remember that luck and knowing people is a big factor in getting hired. For more information on social skills and getting to know people, review chapter 9.

Job Offers

When a company offers you a job, you'll be contacted by either the interviewer or another representative of the company. They will extend an offer to you, including salary and benefits. Make sure the offer is in writing before you accept. If you want to think about the offer before accepting it, give a firm date for when you will contact them—no more than three days after the offer.

Choosing between two great options can be a challenge. One aspect of ADD is indecisiveness, so use the following information to help you make an informed choice.

LOOK AT THE BENEFITS

If you have ADD, you may bypass details and judge a job solely on salary. You may be missing the fine details, like hours and benefits. Benefits are the additional factors that can influence your choice of job. They are just as valuable as salary. Benefits include medical insurance, dental insurance, life insurance, retirement plans, access to corporate fitness centers, and paid leave.

Health insurance. When reviewing your benefits, pay attention to whether the company offers preferred provider medical insurance (PPO) or managed care medical insurance (HMO). In general, PPOs are more expensive, but they typically provide better coverage and easier access to more doctors. You may also want to look specifically at a company's mental health benefits, which may be much more restricted than other medical benefits.

Retirement accounts. Since people with ADD have difficulty planning for the future, they don't really consider that one day they will retire and live off of their savings. If your job offers you retirement accounts like an IRA or 401(k), put the maximum amount of money in every month—this is money that you legally put away without paying taxes on it. Even if you have to cut corners in other areas, make sure you put as much money in those accounts as possible.

Potential for advancement. If you continue to work at the company, what are the chances of you advancing in position and salary? You may have been given this information during the interview; however, if you know some of the employees personally, you can ask them how long they've worked at the company, what jobs they've held there, and how long it took them to advance to the next level. While you're talking with employees, ask them about the atmosphere and culture of the company. Is it conservative or relaxed? Is there a dress code? Are the hours flexible?

Location, location, location. How important is it that you stay close to your family? If you've lived in a warm climate, will you be able to adjust to colder temperatures? People with ADD have difficulty with transitions, so you want this big change to be as smooth as possible. If your job requires that you move, negotiate moving costs with the company, and think through how the transition is likely to affect you.

Making a Job Choice

If you are having difficulty choosing between two jobs, fill out the following worksheet to help you come to a decision. Because you received a job offer in writing, you should already have information on your income, work location, tuition reimbursement, medical insurance, retirement plan, and leave. If you don't have this information, contact the person who offered you the job and ask that he or she add this new information to your written job offer. For more information about the prospective employer, you can also search their website and research their stock history on any financial news website.

Job #1

Income _____

Work atmosphere _____

Security/stability of job _____

Work location _____

Commuting time _____

Advancement
opportunities _____

Tuition reimbursement _____

Medical insurance

     Type: ☐ HMO ☐ PPO

Retirement plan _____

     Will your employer
     match funds? _____

Paid leave _____

Job #2

Income _____

Work atmosphere _____

Security/stability of job _____

Work location _____

Commuting time _____

Advancement
opportunities _____

Tuition reimbursement _____

Medical insurance

     Type: ☐ HMO ☐ PPO

Retirement plan _____

     Will your employer
     match funds? _____

Paid leave _____

Learn the art of negotiation. It has been said that everything in life is up for negotiation—including benefits. You have a right to ask for more money or a better benefits package. If you have more than one employer seeking to hire you, you can ask one employer to improve on the benefits and salary offered by the other employer. You can find more information on the art of negotiating in the Resources section.

BE REALISTIC

When you have ADD, you may be prone to catch the "Why am I not a CEO right out of college?" bug. You want to bypass the years of work and get to the good stuff. That's because people with ADD have a problem with *delayed gratification*. It's hard working toward a goal when that goal seems far away. Keep in mind that the first job you get out of school may not pay a lot, and it may not be exactly what you are looking for. Make the best of it, and your opportunities for advancement will increase. But also make sure that it's a job that fits you—one that optimizes your abilities and minimizes your weaknesses.

And, even if your first job is, shall we say, lacking in the salary department, you still have financial obligations. One of those obligations is to start paying back your student loans.

It's Payback Time

Let's say you have student loans. A lot of students do. And graduation means paying those loans back. But wait! For a period of six months after you graduate, you are not required to make any monthly payments on your loans.

You'll hear all about the grace period and repayment process at your student loan exit interview, either at your college or online, before you graduate. The exit interview includes an explanation of the repayment process, repayment options, and an overview of the National Student Loan Data System (NSLDS), where you can look up your loan online. Most important, you'll find out your monthly payment amount.

No special accommodations can help you repay your student loans; producing a letter that says you have ADD and have poor money management skills will not get you out of paying your loans. However, when paying back your student loans, you may be able to get a decrease in the interest percentage if you pay through electronic withdrawal. Electronic withdrawal also means less work for you and one less bill to remember. You may also be able to consolidate your loans, or combine them for a lower interest rate.

DEFERMENTS AND FORBEARANCE

You can get a loan *deferment*, or temporary stop on loan payments, if you are attending graduate school, if you are unemployed (for up to three years), or if you can show economic hardship. You can also get a *forbearance*, allowing you to temporarily stop loan payments, pay the interest only, or make a payment for lower than the usual amount due. Your loan will still accrue interest during forbearance. To learn more information about deferments or forbearance, see the Resources section at the end of this book.

Conclusion

As you've learned from this book, you can have a rewarding and successful college experience. Remember that asking for help is a sign of strength rather than weakness. You are not alone—your family and friends still love, care for, and support you, even when they are miles away. In fact, you are now a part of two communities—one in your hometown and one at your college. How cool is that?

You may feel challenged at times, and you may have moments where you just want to quit college and move back home. When you start feeling like this, close your eyes and visualize yourself at graduation, in your cap and gown, receiving your diploma. All the work will be worth it.

You have reached the end of the book. Congratulations! You are now an expert on college and ADD. Go forth, make good grades, and have a great time.

Resources

ADDICTION

Alcoholics Anonymous
www.alcoholics-anonymous.org

Narcotics Anonymous
www.na.org

ADULT ADD

Attention Deficit Disorder Association
www.add.org

Children and Adults with Attention-Deficit/Hyperactivity Disorder
(CHADD)
www.chadd.org

Hallowell, E., and J. Ratey. 2005. *Delivered from Distraction: Getting the Most Out of Life with Attention Deficit Disorder.* New York: Ballantine Books.

Weiss, L. 2005. *Attention Deficit Disorder in Adults: A Different Way of Thinking.* 4th ed. New York: Taylor Trade Publishing.

AUTOMOBILE SAFETY

American Automobile Association
800-222-1134
www.aaa.com

BICYCLE SAFETY ON CAMPUS

Bicycle Helmet Safety Institute
www.helmets.org/camptips.htm

Mid-America Regional Council
www.marc.org/bikeped/college.htm

BUSINESS ETIQUETTE

Post, P. 2005. *Emily Post's The Etiquette Advantage in Business: Personal Skills for Professional Success.* 2nd ed. New York: Collins.

Round Lake Publishing Company. 2000. *The Book of Contemporary Business Letters.* 4th ed. Ridgefield, CT: Author.

CAMPUS CRIME STATISTICS

The Chronicle of Higher Education
www.chronicle.com/stats/crime

CANADIAN STUDENT RIGHTS

Canadian National Educational Association of Disabled Students
www.neads.ca

CAREER INFORMATION

Monster
www.monster.com

U.S. Department of Labor, Bureau of Labor Statistics. *Occupational Outlook Handbook.*
www.bls.gov/oco

CHOOSING A MAJOR

Nadler, B. 2006. *The Everything College Major Test Book: 10 Tests to Help You Choose the Major That Is Right for You.* Cincinnati, OH: Adams Media Corporation.

CLINICAL TRIALS

CenterWatch
www.centerwatch.com

National Institute of Mental Health
www.nimh.nih.gov/health/trials

U.S. National Institutes of Health
www.clinicaltrials.gov

COACHING

ADD Consults
www.addconsults.com/coaches

COLLEGE AND ADD

Kravets, M., and I. F. Wax. 2007. *The K & W Guide to Colleges for Students with Learning Disabilities or Attention Deficit/Hyperactivity Disorder (ADHD).* 9th ed. New York: Princeton Review.

Nadeau, K. G. 2006. *Survival Guide for College Students with ADHD or LD.* 2nd ed. Washington, DC: Magination Press.

Quinn, P. O., ed. 2001. *ADD and the College Student: A Guide for High School and College Students with Attention Deficit Disorder.* Rev. ed. Washington, DC: Magination Press.

"Web Resources for Assisting College Students with Disabilities"
http://das.kucrl.org/iam/resources.html

COLLEGE APPLICATIONS

Long, E. 2007. *College Applicant Organizer: The Essential Tool for Applying to College.* Portland, ME: Sellers Publishing.

Rankin, E., and B. Murphy. 2005. *McGraw-Hill's Writing an Outstanding College Application Essay.* New York: McGraw-Hill.

COLLEGE FINDERS

CollegeBoard.com, "College Matchmaker"
http://collegesearch.collegeboard.com/search/index.jsp

Federal Student Aid, "College Matching Wizard"
https://studentaid2.ed.gov/gotocollege/collegefinder/wizard_intro1.asp

Federal Student Aid, "College Finder"
https://studentaid2.ed.gov/gotocollege/CollegeFinder/advanced_find.asp

COLLEGE SUCCESS

Ellis, S. 2003. *Becoming a Master Student.* 10th ed. Boston: Houghton Mifflin Company.

Nist-Olejnik, S., and J. P. Holschuh. 2007. *College Rules! How to Study, Survive, and Succeed in College.* 2nd ed. Berkeley, CA: Ten Speed Press.

Tyler, S. 2001. *Been There, Should Have Done That II: More Tips for Making the Most of College.* Haslett, MI: Front Porch Press.

CO-OPS

North American Students of Cooperation
www.nasco.coop

CREDIT CARD DEBT

National Foundation for Credit Counseling
www.nfcc.org

DATA BACKUP

IBackup
www.ibackup.com
Xdrive
www.xdrive.com

DEPRESSION AND ANXIETY

Anxiety Disorders Association of America
www.adaa.org

Depression and Bipolar Support Alliance
www.ndmda.org

DISCRIMINATION IN THE WORKPLACE

Equal Employment Opportunity Commission (EEOC)
800-669-4000
www.eeoc.gov

EATING DISORDERS

National Eating Disorders Association
www.edap.org

FINANCIAL AID INFORMATION

Federal Student Aid Information Center
800-4-FED-AID (800-433-3243)
www.studentaid.ed.gov

Federal Student Aid website on deferments and forbearance
www.ed.gov/DirectLoan/avoid.html

Financial Aid Information Page
www.finaid.org

Free Application for Student Aid (FAFSA)
800-4-FED-AID (800-433-3243)
www.fafsa.ed.gov

HEATH Resource Center
George Washington University
202-973-0904
www.heath.gwu.edu

National Association of Student Financial Aid Administrators
www.nasfaa.org

Nellie Mae
www.nelliemae.com

FRATERNITIES AND SORORITIES

GreekChat
www.greekchat.com

National Panhellenic Conference
www.npcwomen.org

North-American Interfraternity Conference
www.nicindy.org

GRANTS

U.S. Department of Education
Federal Pell Grant Program
www.ed.gov/programs/fpg

U.S. Department of Education
Academic Competitiveness (AC) Grants
National Science and Mathematics Access to Retain Talent
(SMART) Grants
www.ed.gov/about/inits/ed/competitiveness/ac-smart2.html

LABELING MACHINES

Brother
  www.brother.com

DYMO
  www.dymo.com

LAPTOP SECURITY LOCKS

Kensington Computer Products Group
  www.kensington.com

LOAN FORGIVENESS

FinAid
  www.finaid.org/loans/forgiveness.phtml

MEDICATION

National Alliance on Mental Illness
  www.nami.org

National Resource Center on AD/HD, "Medication Management for Adults with ADHD"
  www.addresources.org/article_adhd_medication_chadd.php

Pharmaceutical Companies' Sites

CONCERTA
www.concerta.net

Daytrana
www.daytrana.com

Strattera
www.strattera.com

Vyvanse
www.vyvanse.com

MONEY MANAGEMENT INFORMATION

Young Money
www.youngmoney.com

Orman, S. 2007. *The Money Book for the Young, Fabulous, and Broke.* New York: Riverhead Trade.

MONEY MANAGEMENT SOFTWARE/INTERNET

Buxfer (free software designed for college students by college students) www.buxfer.com

Quicken
www.quicken.com

NEGOTIATION

Fisher, R., and D. Ertel. 1995. *Getting Ready to Negotiate: The Getting to Yes Workbook.* New York: Penguin Books.

Fisher, R., B. Patton, and W. Ury. 1991. *Getting to Yes: Negotiating Agreement without Giving In.* New York: Penguin Books.

NETWORKING

Fisher, D., and S. Vilas. 2000. *Power Networking: 55 Secrets for Personal and Professional Success.* 2nd ed. Houston: Bard Books.

ORGANIZATION PRODUCTS

Stacks and Stacks
www.stacksandstacks.com

Target
www.target.com

PASSWORD STORAGE

Agatra
www.agatra.com

KeePass
www.keepass.info/download.html

Password Depot
www.password-depot.com

PROFESSOR RATINGS

ProfRater.com
www.profrater.com

Rate My Professors
www.ratemyprofessors.com

SCHOLARSHIP SEARCH

Canadian Scholarships
www.studentawards.com

College Answer
www.collegeanswer.com

College Board
www.collegeboard.org

Financial Aid Search Through the Web (FastWeb)
www.fastweb.com

Stafford Loans
www.staffordloans.com

U.S. Department of Education
800-433-3243
www.ed.gov

SOCIAL NETWORKING WEBSITE

Facebook
www.facebook.com

SOCIAL SKILLS

Novotni, M. 2001. *What Does Everyone Know That I Don't? Social Skills Help for Adults with Attention Deficit/Hyperactivity Disorder (AD/HD).* Plantation, FL: Specialty Press.

Post, P. 2004. *Emily Post's Etiquette.* 17th ed. New York: Harper Resource.

STANDARDIZED TESTING

Graduate Record Examinations (GRE)
www.ets.org/gre

Law School Admission Test (LSAT)
Law School Admission Council
www.lsac.org

Medical College Admission Test (MCAT)
ADHD Accommodation Guidelines
www.aamc.org/students/mcat/adhd.pdf

STUDENT RIGHTS AND LAWS

Family Educational Rights and Privacy Act (FERPA)
U.S. Department of Education
www.ed.gov/policy/gen/guid/fpco/ferpa

HEATH Resource Center
Online Clearinghouse on Postsecondary Education for Individuals with Disabilities
www.heath.gwu.edu

Office for Civil Rights
U.S. Department of Education
Washington, DC 20202-1100
800-421-3481
877-521-2172 (TDD)
ocr@ed.gov (e-mail)
www.ed.gov/ocr

"Students with Disabilities Preparing for Postsecondary Education: Know Your Rights and Responsibilities"
www.ed.gov/about/offices/list/ocr/transition.html

"How to File a Discrimination Complaint with the Office for Civil Rights"
www.ed.gov/ocr/docs/howto.html

Wrightslaw
www.wrightslaw.com

STUDY SKILLS AND TEST-TAKING

HowtoStudy.org
www.howtostudy.org

Study Guides and Strategies
www.studygs.net

LearningExpress. 2007. *Test-Taking Power Strategies: Improve Your Test Scores.* New York: Author.

Newport, C. 2006. *How to Become a Straight-A Student: The Unconventional Strategies Real College Students Use to Score High While Studying Less.* New York: Broadway Books.

SUICIDE

National Suicide Prevention Lifeline
800-273-TALK (8255)

TYPING SKILLS

Typing Test
www.typingtest.com

PowerTyping
www.powertyping.com

VOICE RECOGNITION SOFTWARE

Dragon NaturallySpeaking
www.nuance.com/naturallyspeaking

WHITE NOISE AIDS

Marpac Corporation
www.marpac.com

Pure White Noise CDs
www.purewhitenoise.com

References

Abraham, A., S. Windmann, R. Siefen, I. Daum, and O. Güntürkün. 2006. Creative thinking in adolescents with attention deficit hyperactivity disorder (ADHD). *Child Neuropsychology* 12(2):111–23.

American Council on Education. 2006. Missed opportunities revisited: New information on students who do not apply for financial aid. *ACE Issue Brief*, 1–16.

Americans with Disabilities Act, Public Law 101-336, *U.S. Code* 42, § 12181 et seq.

———. Title II, § 202.

Antalis, C. J., L. J. Stevens, M. Campbell, R. Pazdro, K. Ericson, and J. R. Burgess. 2006. Omega-3 fatty acid status in attention-deficit/hyperactivity disorder. *Prostaglandins, Leukotrienes and Essential Fatty Acids* 75(4–5):299–308.

Barkley, R.A. 2006. Driving risks in adults with ADD: Yet more evidence and a personal story. *ADD Report* 14(5):1–9.

Barkley, R. A., M. Fischer, L. Smallish, and K. Fletcher. 2005. Young adult outcome of hyperactive children: Adaptive functioning in major life activities. *Journal of the American Academy of Child and Adolescent Psychiatry* 45(2):192–202.

Barkley, R. A., K. R. Murphy, T. O'Connell, D. Anderson, and D. F. Connor. 2006. Effects of two doses of alcohol on simulator driving performance in adults with attention deficit hyperactivity disorder. *Neuropsychology* 20(1):77–87.

Barkley, R. A., K. R. Murphy, T. O'Connell, and D. F. Connor. 2005. Effects of two doses of methylphenidate on simulator driving performance in adults with attention deficit hyperactivity disorder. *Journal of Safety Research* 36(2):121–31.

Beebe, D. W., C. T. Wells, J. Jeffries, B. Chini, M. Kalra, and R. Amin. 2004. Neuropsychological effects of pediatric obstructive sleep apnea. *Journal of the International Neuropsychological Society* 10(7):962–75.

Biederman, J. 2003. Pharmacotherapy for attention-deficit/hyperactivity disorder (ADHD) decreases the risk for substance abuse: Findings from a longitudinal follow-up of youths with and without ADHD. *Journal of Clinical Psychiatry* 64(Suppl. 11):3–8.

Biederman, J., S. W. Ball, M. C. Monuteaux, C. B. Surman, J. L. Johnson, and S. Zeitlin. 2007. Are girls with ADHD at risk for eating disorders? Results from a controlled, five-year prospective study. *Journal of Developmental and Behavioral Pediatrics* 28(4):302–7.

Biederman, J., M. C. Monuteaux, E. Mick, T. E. Wilens, J. A. Fontanella, K. M. Poetzl, T. Kirk, J. Masse, and S. V. Faraone. 2006. Is cigarette smoking a gateway to alcohol and illicit drug use disorders? A study of youths with and without attention deficit hyperactivity disorder. *Biological Psychiatry* 59(3):258–64.

Cox, D. J., M. Punja, K. Powers, R. L. Merkel, R. Burket, M. Moore, R. Thhorndike, and B. Kovatchev. 2006. Manual transmission enhances attention and driving performance of ADD adolescent males: Pilot study. *Journal of Attention Disorders* 10(2):212–16.

Curtis, P., and S. Gaylord. 2005. Safety issues in the interaction of conventional, complementary, and alternative health care. *Complementary Health Practice Review* 10(1):3-31.

Davis, C., R. D. Levitan, M. Smith, S. Tweed, and C. Curtis. 2006. Associations among overeating, overweight, and attention deficit/hyperactivity disorder: A structural equation modeling approach. *Eating Behaviors* 7(3):266–74.

Eisenberg, D., E. Golberstein, and S. E. Gollust. 2007. Help-seeking and access to mental health care in a university student population. *Medical Care* 45(7):594–601.

Ellenbogen, J., J. Hulbert, R. Stickgold, D. Dinges, and S. Thompson-Schill. 2006. Interfering with theories of sleep and memory: Sleep, declarative memory, and associative interference. *Current Biology.* 16(3):1290–94.

Faraone, S. V., J. Biederman, T. E. Wilens, and J. Adamson. 2007. A naturalistic study of the effects of pharmacotherapy on substance use disorders among ADHD adults. *Psychological Medicine* 37(12):1743–52.

Fischer, A. G., C. H. Bau, E. H. Grevet, C. A. Salgado, M. M. Victor, K. L. Kalil, N. O. Sousa, C. R. Garcia, and P. Belmonte-de-Abreu. 2007. The role of comorbid major depressive disorder in the clinical presentation of adult ADHD. *Journal of Psychiatric Research* 41(12):991–96.

Fischer, M., R. A. Barkley, L. Smallish, and K. Fletcher. 2007. Hyperactive children as young adults: Driving abilities, safe driving behavior, and adverse driving outcomes. *Accident Analysis and Prevention* 39(1):94–105.

Fisher, B., F. Cullen, and M. Turner. 2000. *The Sexual Victimization of College Women.* Washington, DC: U.S. Department of Justice, National Institute of Justice and Bureau of Justice Statistics.

Flory, K., B. S. Molina, W. E. Pelham, E. Gnagy, and B. Smith. 2006. Childhood ADD predicts risky sexual behavior in young adulthood. *Journal of Clinical Child and Adolescent Psychology* 35(4):571–77.

Fried, R., C. R. Petty, C. B. Surman, B. Reimer, M. Aleardi, J. M. Martin, J. F. Coughlin, and J. Biederman. 2006. Characterizing impaired driving in adults with attention-deficit/hyperactivity disorder: A controlled study. *Journal of Clinical Psychiatry* 67(4):567–74.

Gau, S. S., R. C. Kessler, W. L. Tseng, Y. Y. Wu, Y. N. Chiu, C. B. Yeh, and H. G. Hwu. 2007. Association between sleep problems and symptoms of attention-deficit/hyperactivity disorder in young adults. *Sleep* 30(2):195–201.

Kessler, R. C., L. Adler, R. Barkley, J. Biederman, C. K. Conners, O. Demler, S. V. Faraone, et al. 2006. The prevalence and correlates of adult ADHD in the United States: Results from the National Comorbidity Survey Replication. *American Journal of Psychiatry* 163(4):716–23.

Kollins, S. H., F. J. McClernon, and B. F. Fuemmeler. 2005. Association between smoking and attention-deficit/hyperactivity disorder symptoms in a population-based sample of young adults. *Archives of General Psychiatry* 62(10):1142–47.

Levin, J. R., S. M. Evans, D. J. Brooks, and F. Garawi. 2007. Treatment of cocaine dependent treatment seekers with adult ADHD: Double-blind comparison of methylphenidate and placebo. *Drug and Alcohol Dependence* 87(1):20–29.

Levitsky, D. A., C. A. Halbmaier, and G. Mrdjenovic. 2004. The freshman weight gain: A model for the study of the epidemic of obesity. *International Journal of Obesity* 28(11):1435–42.

Mackie, S., P. Shaw, R. Lenroot, R. Pierson, D. K. Greenstein, T. F. Nugent III, W. S. Sharp, J. N. Giedd, and J. L. Rapoport. 2007. Cerebellar development and clinical outcome in attention deficit hyperactivity disorder. *American Journal of Psychiatry* 164(4):647–55.

Mattos, P., E. Saboya, V. Ayrão, D. Segenreich, M. Duchesne, and G. Coutinho. 2004. Comorbid eating disorders in a Brazilian attention-deficit/hyperactivity disorder adult clinical sample. *Revista Brasileira de Psiquiatria* 26(4):248–50.

Matza, L. S., C. Paramore, and M. Prasad. 2005. A review of the economic burden of ADHD. *Cost Effectiveness and Resource Allocation* 3(June 9):5.

McCabe, S., C. Teter, and C. Boyd. 2006. Medical use, illicit use, and diversion of prescription stimulant medication. *Journal of Psychoactive Drugs* 38(1):43–56.

McEvoy, P. M. 2007. Effectiveness of cognitive behavioural group therapy for social phobia in a community clinic: A benchmarking study. *Behaviour Research and Therapy* 75(2):344–50.

Nellie Mae. 2005. *Undergraduate Students and Credit Cards in 2004: An Analysis of Usage Rates and Trends*. Braintree, MA: Author.

Norvilitis, J. M. 2002. Credit card debt on college campuses: Causes, consequences, and solutions. *College Student Journal* (September).

Parks, K. A., and W. Fals-Stewart. 2004. The temporal relationship between college women's alcohol consumption and victimization experiences. *Alcoholism: Clinical and Experimental Research* 28(4):625–29.

Parsons, T. J., O. Manor, and C. Power. 2007. Television viewing and obesity: A prospective study in the 1958 British birth cohort. *European Journal of Clinical Nutrition* (August 22). http://www.nature.com/ejen.

Poulin, C. 2007. From attention-deficit/hyperactivity disorder to medical stimulant use to the diversion of prescribed stimulants to non-medical stimulant use: Connecting the dots. *Addiction* 102(5):740–51.

Propper, R. E., R. Stickgold, R. Keeley, and S. D. Christman. 2007. Is television traumatic? Dreams, stress, and media exposure in the aftermath of September 11, 2001. *Psychological Science* 18(4):334–40.

Richards, T., J. Deffenbacher, and L. Rosen. 2002. Driving anger and other driving-related behaviors in high and low ADD symptom college students. *Journal of Attention Disorders* 6(1):25–38.

Rietveld, M. J. H., J. J. Hudziak, M. Bartels, C. E. M. Beijsterveldt, D. I. Boomsma. 2004. Heritability of attention problems in children: Longitudinal results from a study of twins, age 3 to 12. *Journal of Child Psychology and Psychiatry* 45(3):577-88.

Sabuncuoglu, O. 2007. Traumatic dental injuries and attention-deficit/hyperactivity disorder: Is there a link? *Dental Traumatology* 23(3):137–42.

Safren, S. A., P. Duran, I. Yovel, C. A. Perlman, and S. Sprich. 2007. Medication adherence in psychopharmacologically treated adults with ADHD. *Journal of Attention Disorders* 10(3):257–60.

Schredl, M., B. Alm, and E. Sobanski. 2007. Sleep quality in adult patients with attention deficit hyperactivity disorder (ADHD). *European Archives of Psychiatry and Clinical Neuroscience* 257(3):164–68.

Schuchman, M. 2007. Falling through the cracks: Virginia Tech and the restructuring of college mental health services. *New England Journal of Medicine* 357(2):105–10.

Schwartz, A. J. 2006. College student suicide in the United States: 1990–1991 through 2003–2004. *Journal of American College Health* 54(6):341–52.

Shaw-Zirt, B., L. Popali-Lehane, W. Chaplin, and A. Bergman. 2005. Adjustment, social skills, and self-esteem in college students with symptoms of ADHD. *Journal of Attention Disorders* 8(3):109–20.

Sinn, N., and J. Bryan. 2007. Effect of supplementation with polyunsaturated fatty acids and micronutrients on learning and behavior problems associated with child ADHD. *Journal of Developmental and Behavioral Pediatrics* 28(2):82–91.

Smith, S. M., and E. Vela. 2001. Environmental context-dependent memory: A review and meta-analysis. *Psychonomic Bulletin and Review* 8(2):203–20.

Solhkhah, R., T. E. Wilens, J. Daly, J. B. Prince, S. L. Van Patten, and J. Biederman. 2005. Bupropion SR for the treatment of substance-abusing outpatient adolescents with attention-deficit/hyperactivity disorder and mood disorders. *Journal of Child and Adolescent Psychopharmacology* 15(5):777–86.

Thompson, A. L., B. S. Molina, W. Pelham, and E. M. Gnagy. 2007. Risky driving in adolescents and young adults with childhood ADD. *Journal of Pediatric Psychology* 32(7):745–59.

Trammell, J. K. 2003. The impact of academic accommodations on final grades in a postsecondary setting. *Journal of College Reading and Learning* 34(1):76–90.

U.S. Department of Education, Office for Civil Rights. 2007. *Students with Disabilities Preparing for Postsecondary Education: Know Your Rights and Responsibilities.* Washington, DC: Author.

Van der Heijden, K. B., M. G. Smits, E. J. Van Someren, K. R. Ridderinkhof, and W. B. Gunning. 2007. Effect of melatonin on sleep, behavior, and cognition in ADHD and chronic sleep-onset insomnia. *Journal of the American Academy of Child and Adolescent Psychiatry* 46(2):233–41.

White, A. M., J. D. Jordan, K. M. Schroeder, S. K. Acheson, B. D. Georgi, G. Sauls, R. R. Ellington, H. S. Schwartzwelder. 2004. Predictors of relapse during treatment completion among marijuana-dependent adolescents in an intensive outpatient substance abuse program. *Substance Abuse* 25(1):53-59.

Wilens, T. E. 2004. Attention-deficit/hyperactivity disorder and the substance use disorders: The nature of the relationship, subtypes at risk, and treatment issues. *Psychiatric Clinics of North America* 27(2):283–301.

Wilens, T. E., M. Gignac, A. Swezey, M. C. Monuteaux, and J. Biederman. 2006. Characteristics of adolescents and young adults with ADHD who divert or misuse their prescribed medications. *Journal of the American Academy of Child and Adolescent Psychiatry* 45(4):408–14.

Wilens, T. E., M. C. Monuteaux, L. E. Snyder, H. Moore, J. Whitley, and M. Gignac. 2005. The clinical dilemma of using medications in substance-abusing adolescents and adults with attention-deficit/ hyperactivity disorder: What does the literature tell us? *Journal of Child and Adolescent Psychopharmacology* 15(5):787–98.

Wilens, T. E., and H. P. Upadhyaya. 2007. Impact of substance use disorder on ADHD and its treatment. *Journal of Clinical Psychiatry* 68(8):e20.

Wolraich, M. L., C. J. Wibbelsman, T. E. Brown, S. W. Evans, E. M. Gotlieb, J. R. Knight, E. C. Ross, H. H. Shubiner, E. H. Wender, and T. Wilens. 2005. Attention-deficit/hyperactivity disorder among adolescents: A review of the diagnosis, treatment, and clinical implications. *Pediatrics* 115(6):1734–46.

Yeghiayan, S. K., J. H. Georgelis, T. J. Maher, and H. R. Lieberman. 2004. Beneficial effects of a protein free, high carbohydrate meal on rat coping behavior and neurotransmitter levels during heat stress. *Nutritional Neuroscience* 7(5/6):335-40.

Yen, J. Y., C. H. Ko, C. F. Yen, H. Y. Wu, and M. J. Yang. 2007. The comorbid psychiatric symptoms of Internet addiction: Attention deficit and hyperactivity disorder (ADHD), depression, social phobia, and hostility. *Journal of Adolescent Health* 41(1):93–98.

Young, G. S., J. A. Conquer, and R. Thomas. 2005. Effect of supplementation with polyunsaturated fatty acids and micronutrients on learning and behavior problems associated with child ADHD. *Reproduction, Nutrition, Development* 45(5):549–58.

Index

Stephanie Moulton Sarkis, Ph.D., is a national certified counselor and licensed mental health counselor in Gainesville, Florida who specializes in ADD counseling and coaching. She is also the director of assessments and evaluations at Sarkis Family Psychiatry and Sarkis Clinical Trials and an assistant adjunct professor at the University of Florida. In 2001, Dr. Sarkis won an American Psychological Association Outstanding Dissertation Award for her research on ADD, brain function, and comorbid disorders. She is the author of *10 Simple Solutions to Adult ADD* and has been featured on national and regional television and radio, including ABC News, Fox News, and CNN. Find Dr. Sarkis online at www.stephaniesarkis.com.

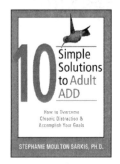